Norbert Szyperski / Erwin Grochla
Ursula M. Richter / Wilfried P. Weitz (Eds.)

Assessing the Impacts of Information Technology

Program Applied Informatics

Editors:
Paul Schmitz
Norbert Szyperski

Wulf Werum / Hans Windauer:
PEARL, Process and Experiment Automation
Realtime Language

Wulf Werum / Hans Windauer:
Introduction to PEARL
Process and Experiment Automation
Realtime Language

Joachim Kanngiesser:
Die Abrechnung von ADV-Systemleistungen

Eric D. Carlson / Wolfgang Metz / Günter Müller /
Ralph H. Sprague / Jimmy A. Sutton:
Display Generation and Management
Systems (DGMS) for Interactive
Business Applications

Bernd Rosenstengel / Udo Winand:
Petri-Netze. Eine anwendungsorientierte
Einführung

Norbert Szyperski / Erwin Grochla / Ursula M. Richter /
Wilfried P. Weitz (Eds.):
Assessing the Impacts of Information Technology

Paul Schmitz / Heinz Bons / Rudolf van Megen:
Software-Qualitätssicherung — Testen im Software-Lebenszyklus

Christina Tiedemann:
Kostenrechnung für Rechenzentren

Norbert Szyperski
Erwin Grochla
Ursula M. Richter
Wilfried P. Weitz (Eds.)

Assessing the Impacts of Information Technology

Hope to escape the negative effects
of an Information Society by Research

Friedr. Vieweg & Sohn   Braunschweig/Wiesbaden

ISBN 978-3-528-03591-4   ISBN 978-3-322-85393-6 (eBook)
DOI 10.1007/978-3-322-85393-6

Table of Contents

PREFACE

The contents of this volume is based upon presentations that took place during the international research symposium "Research on Impacts - Hope for Escaping the Negative Effects of an Information Society" in Walberberg on May 25 - 26, 1981.

The symposium was organized by the Institute for Organization and Automation at the University of Cologne (BIFOA) within a research project on "Konstruktive Wirkungsforschung" and was sponsored by the German Federal Ministry for Research and Technology.

Information technology is considered to be the crucial factor for the future development of our society. The expectations differ widely in respect to how this development will look like. Information technology has on the one hand the potential of causing substantial negative impacts on individuals and on society but on the other hand the potential of being the key technology for solving pressing problems of mankind. The decisions of today will already determine which impacts we have to cope with in the future. The challenge for research is therefore to deliver sufficient information to enable the decision makers to make the right decisions.

The conference was designed to provide an opportunity to exchange ideas on aims and issues of research on technological impacts and especially to discuss the chances to meet this research challenge and to achieve satisfying contributions by research for coping with future impacts of information technology.

In this volume, three parts are distinguished. Part I provides an overview over the objectives, functions, and philosophies of the assessment of information technology. The second part comprised several articles about the practicability, applicability, and the benefits of this kind of research. The question "how to get good research results" is taken up in Part III. It is asked for the best strategy for impact research. Furthermore, this final part contains the discussion of several problematic issues, often demanded as mandatory for achieving good results.

Norbert Szyperski
Erwin Grochla
Ursula Richter
Wilfried P. Weitz

ACKNOWLEDGEMENTS

We are greatly indebted to all participants of our symposium
for their presentations and contributions to the discussions.
We owe considerable thanks to Niels Bjørn-Andersen, Klaus
Haefner and Patrick Johnson who significantly contributed
to the success of the symposium by stimulating and directing
the discussions as chairmen.

We greatly appreciate the sponsorship of the symposium by
the German Federal Ministry for Research and Technology as
well as the encouragement and the active participation of
its representatives. We are especially grateful to the members of GMD-APM, the project management of the Federal Ministry for Research and Technology, who were in charge of our
project and always kindly supported us in solving the financial, organizational and technical problems related to such
a symposium.

A special note of thanks is due to the authors who have been
very helpful in preparing this publication. The editors feel
particular indebted to Niels Bjørn-Anderson for his valuable
suggestions and support in preparing the introductions and
discussion summaries.

We are very grateful to our student assistants, Peter
Kerßenfischer, Susanne Kohout, Helmut Lalla, Gabriele
Pöggeler, Martin Reiß and Klaus Scheimann for their out-
standing cooperation in organizing the symposium and their
editorial assistance.

Finally our thanks go to Ingrid Hacker and Karin Kötz for
their typing efforts and patience.

INTRODUCTION

Our society is a living organism. There is no standstill or freezing in on a certain level of development. But there is a permanent process of change going on. Some changes pass slowly and almost unrecognized. Others again are accompanied by anything from public discussions to vehement fights.

In a historical perspective most of these societal changes represent movements that could be classified as progress or setbacks along a quasi continuous line of societal development. But from time to time in its history society seems to leave its steady path of development and switch over to another path, a quantum jump.

There exist a lot of signs recently that we have reached again such a "Copernican" turning point and that we are already in the middle of the transition process from one kind of society to a dramatically different one.

The need for giving up the development path followed hitherto is to a substantial degree caused by technological "side effects". The limits to growth in a society based on technologies of the industrial era have been reached in several cases. Considered from a more comprehensive point of view the social and ecological costs of further dissemination of technology applications of the industrial era often exceed the expected benefits. More and more new solutions are requested and the actual need for them increases.

The limits of applications of certain technologies which manifest themselves today mainly in threats of almost irreversible ecological damages stirred up the discussion about the necessity and usefulness of modern technologies for the society. The advocates of certain technological progress can point to a lot of good arguments in their favour. But on the other hand the technology opponents are not at all at a loss for reasons to support their conviction. Considering all kinds of arguments[1] both directions along the traditional path of development seem to be dead ends. So the only solution open while pursuing the goal of a better quality of life for more people appears to be a new societal orientation.

Having left the traditional path of development implies for the society the abandonment of certain states of stability and security. The degree of uncertainty within the transition society is increased. The fan of possible futures broadens tremendously. Prognoses based on extrapolation must fail in such situations. But within this higher level of uncertainty there stands out one fact: The new society we are heading for will rely on technologies even more than the old one. And there is little doubt that the technology most important in shaping our future society will be the information technology.

The problem we have to deal with is therefore not one of "more or less technology". Instead it is a question about a selection between a series of technologies which will secure future societal progress.

The future of a society dominated by information technology has already been described in numerous scenarios. These scenarios, whether scientific prognoses or fiction, show quite different pictures of our future world. The optimistic view

---

1) For a detailed discussion of the "technology and society" problem see e.g. Bereano, P.L.: Technology as a Social and Political Phenomenon. New York: John Wiley & Sons 1976.

presents a society where information technology is used to overcome our current problems concerning food, energy and ecological challenges. Some of the more pessimistic scenarios include these solutions for our elementary needs but point out human menaces of a higher order associated with many of these solutions. Their future society is characterized by the use of information technology to set up a perfect system for surveillance and oppression of the individual citizen.

None of these scenarios is our inescapable future. But we must be aware that our decisions of today will tie us to certain development lines and diminish the fan of possible futures. In such situations an anticipative behavior has to be demanded. In order to shape actively the future the decisions have to be done at a time where the determinants can still be influenced easily. The recent experiences with impacts of technology applications have clarified that a lot more of those existing high complex relationships between technology and society and vice versa have to be taken into account. More efforts must be spent in advance to inquire into all imaginable (mis-)usages of the technology in question and its impacts, even though they appear today very unrealistic.

Many concerned people today request investigations into all possible dangers and negative impacts. That is indeed very important. But likewise the potential inherent in technology applications have to be found out. It is an interesting phenomenon that most people are attracted by visions of dangers and threat. Considering or accentuating only the gloomy perspectives for our possible future contains the great danger of getting stuck in a reactive behavior. This behavior is anticipative too in the sense that one reacts to events before they actually happen. But this does not suffice in order to achieve any progress. The challenge consequently is to discover and minimize the risks, while at the same time exploit the potentials.

This is not an easy task and may not end with the identification of the impacts. The impacts have to be assessed, what turns out to be very difficult to do, because many problem layers have to taken into account.

There seems to exist a basic imbalance in the distribution of benefits and risks. Benefits and negative impacts often appear with different groups or in places which are different in time and space. Do we have to deal with a zero-sum-impact-game? Or is it more the question of finding the right strategies or the need of changing the rules and constraints to achieve positive payoffs for all parties at all times?

The symposium was concerned with the question whether and how research, especially Technology Assessment, can meet this challenge. The main interest was not directed towards the problem what the real impacts of information technology will be. It consisted rather in the discussion of limits, possibilities and strategies of research in this field.

The amount of different names and directions gives already an indication that there does not exist a clearly defined comprehension of research on technological impacts. Does it mean a science, or is it research more like marketing investigations. What should be the result of such research, background information for interested parties or propositions for decisions. Should it be "objective" research, considering all point of views, or should it be "advocacy" research, in the sense that the researcher look like advocates after the interest of those groups, who otherwise cannot support their opinion with the necessary force.

Besides all these questions concerning the "what should be" one might ask "what can actually be achieved".

The standards set for impact research are very high. The research practice shows that they can hardly be reached. Many of these problems, impact research has to face, are representative of almost all kind of research. But the very specific characteristics of impact research tremendously intensify these difficulties. Impact research means investigation into future events and into extremely complex relationships. It means having to cope with often opposite interests of the parties involved and to consider unknown value developments in the assessment.

The gap between the general demands from different interest groups and that what is actually achievable has already been subject of discussions in the Technology Assessment society. It was aim of the symposium to take up the discussion, to elaborate the specialties of research on impacts of information technologies, and to find out whether this research approach is necessary and useful in order to escape the pessimistic scenarios of our information technology based future.

The careful reader will not find a coherent perspective throughout all the contributions. This was not our objective either. Rather we intended to bring in a large variety of different perspectives in order to stimulate discussion and research in the field.

Research on Impacts of Technologies

-Objectives, Functions, and Philosophies-

Anyone setting out to do research on technological impacts soon reaches a state of confusion. The whole idea of impact research is to bring investigations of technological impacts to a higher level of complexity, to wider areas, to bring in new perspectives, and especially to do investigations about the future. That is bound to raise a vast number of problems and to encompass a variety of research perspectives. Therefore it is understandable that a lot of different terms and research directions exist with no clear definition and coordination.

Which one of these research approaches should be followed to achieve the results which best support the goal of making responsible and correct decisions about future technology developments and applications?

The "Establishment" in the United States of America answered the growing concern about the need for more and better ex-ante mastering of technological impacts and well articulated protests from environmental groups with the establishment of the Office of Technology Assessment and the promotion of technology assessment studies sponsored by government agencies. In other countries impact research has been integrated into technological development projects sponsored by research foundations. However, this greater concern and funding has not brought consensus about the best way to pursue common research objectives.

The first part of this conference was dedicated to the discussion of different research approaches. It was intended to give an overview over some objectives, functions and philosophies of research on technological impacts and to clarify their relationships to information technology.

The three papers presented in this session, were "Technology Assessment: Some Aspects Related to Information Technology" by Vary T. Coates, "Social Science Research about the Consequences of Modern Information Technologies" by Renate Mayntz, and "Impact Research and Research Policy - An Analytical Framework" by Jürgen Reese and Bernd-Peter Lange. These papers introduced the subject, illustrated the state of the art, and pointed out the important perspectives related to this kind of research.

The discussion in this first session concentrated on issues of the actual demand for impact research and its utility. A brief summary of the discussion follows.

Information technology has so far not received great attention as an area for technology assessment. The reason for that is not a lack of objective need but a lack of interest expressed by the public. One might roughly identify three consumers of technology assessment studies: citizens, industry, and government. A fourth party, the researchers, shall be neglected in the following.

The demand by citizens for technology assessments is currently directed more toward other kinds of technologies than information technology. There is no widespread consciousness about the importance of information technology for our future life as most of the potential hazards are indirect and far more difficult to communicate than, e.g., the melting down of a nuclear reactor. The call for assessments of information technology, therefore, does not come from the citizens.

The industry seems to have no clear position about technology assessment. On the one hand technology assessments lead to delays and increased costs. On the other hand it is necessary for companies to look ahead and to anticipate the kind of goods and services they are asked to provide in the future in order to survive. From this point of view technology assessment can be an important tool supporting strategic decisions.

The government is the party currently most interested in comprehensive technology assessment studies. Governmental decision-makers need studies showing the direction of different technological developments which clarify the long-term implications of these developments for society.

Technology assessments, therefore, primarily support governments in their planning and policy making. While technology assessment does not deliver final decisions, the utility of assessment studies is in raising wider and often unforeseen issues, in pointing out uncertainties, and in clarifying the crossroads where selections between alternatives have to be made.

Probably one of the most important functions of technology assessment is the translation function. Political decisions have to be made on highly technical issues which are far-reaching and long-termed in their consequences. To maintain the pluralistic democratic nature of Western societies these technical decisions have to be translated into a set of political and social issues. Only then can the affected parties participate in the discussion and politicians find a basis for their decisions.

The results rendered by technology assessment can be very specific (whether or not to launch a TV-satellite) or they may be very broad. An example of the latter is the large study in the USA called "The Global 2000 Report to the President". While the effects of specific research are more direct and visible, more comprehensive studies tend to initiate or stimulate public discussions but have no immediate effect on decision making.

Vary T. Coates

Technology Assessment: Some Aspects Related to Information
Technology

It has been fifteen years since the introduction of the concept of technology assessment. During that time the concept has evolved through experience and shared learning. I will summarize some of those changes, emphasizing the many kinds of assessment programs which have developed. To relate these remarks to the assessment of the impacts of information technology I suggest five characteristics of information technology which could guide the search for potential impacts.

In the first eight to ten years of the development of technology assessment, the emphasis was on "early warning" of potential environmental problems and public health catastrophes. There was an implicit expectation that technology assessment would develop into a new "meta-discipline," a body of fully transferable methods and theorems which would allow us to consistently and reliably forecast impacts.

Technology assessment has since evolved into a more general and useful attitude toward public decisionmaking: it is aimed at prudent management under conditions of uncertainty and at the comparison of alternative paths to maximum societal benefits from technology. This approach strives for systematic and thorough attention to behavioral and institutional reactions and accommodations which may occur in response to technological change, attention to converging societal trends and unexpected exogenous events which condition outcomes, and attention to integration of both quantitative data and qualitative, experiential wisdom.

Technology assessment, in other words, now is recognized as not one research algorithm or model but as a varied palette of analytical and speculative techniques used in support of public policy formulation and strategic planning.

In exploring the possible impacts of technological change, some common elements which have endured and been strenghtened over fifteen years of experience, are:

o interdisciplinarity and integrated analysis

o orientation toward the future and toward multiple possibilities and alternative paths

o an emphasis on discerning the indirect, unintended consequences of technological change

o the primary objective of informing and improving public decisionmaking and policy formulation.

What has newly developed during this experience is:

o increased emphasis on early identification of opportunities as well as problems

o a fuller appreciation of the value of the insights of potentially affected parties and interest groups

o much greater attention to tailoring the assessment to fit the needs and the practical constraints of the political process.

There is in the United States considerable difference in technology assessments done by or for the Office of Technology Assessment, which serves the Congress; the mission agencies of the Executive branch of the Federal government; the National Science Foundation; state governments; special national commissions; and industry. These differences derive primarily from differences in the power, scope, and responsibilities of the decisionmakers whom the assessments are intended to serve, and the characteristic timing and other constraints on decisionmaking. These differences outweigh those stemming from variations in funding level, subject matter, or performers (in contrast to sponsors or users) of the assessment - i.e., university groups, research organizations, in-house staffs, or consultants.

Technology assessment in Federal Executive Agencies has been sporadic, fragmented, narrow, and inadequate. There are of course exceptions. But the agencies are constrained by narrowly framed legislative responsibilities, by internal bureaucratic organization which disperses responsibilities related to any one technology among many process and procedural jurisdictions within an agency, and by the agency's fear of offending special constituencies. Basic decisions are often determined by the Administration's overall political program regardless of assessment outcomes. Nevertheless, impact analysis is playing a strong role in evolution of long-term policy and in R&D budget planning and allocation. The most common characteristic of mission agency assessments, however, is that each agency emphasizes only the impacts within its own area of responsibility -- e.g., environmental impacts, economic development impacts, energy impacts.

The Congressional Office of Technology Assessment, which began operating only eight years ago, struggles to respond to two different needs of the legislature. The first is the need, made explicit in OTA's legislative charter, for a long-range view of developing technological issues and an "early warning" of environmental and social problems. The second - and in practice more imperative - need of the Congress is for a source of scientific and technical information, independent of the Executive agencies, focused on immediate policy issues. This need of course stems from the peculiar characteristics of the American political system as compared to parliamentary systems -- separation of powers between the two branches of government, two-party government, and a fixed electoral cycle. The need for independent advice to compare with Executive agency budgetary justifications was in fact a major factor in the establishment of OTA.

OTA's assessments therefore tend to be less exploratory and more short range than many of us would prefer. The work emphasizes recognized policy issues but de-emphasizes the search for unrecognized potential impacts. It is too often framed around limited technical problems. However, because OTA's clients - the decisionmakers who are to use the assessment - are clearly known and directly receive the results, the assessments have a high probability of being useful. In the last several years, OTA has also been very successful in seeking and using public participation in many of its assessments.

Unlike Executive agencies, which usually have assessments done by contractors, OTA does much of the integrating analysis in-house, to keep it in close contact with developing policy issues and Congressional committee needs. In spite of this, a major problem is that good assessments take a long time. Timely response to swiftly moving policy developments has often not been possible.

The National Science Foundation was the earliest source of technology assessment sponsorship, beginning about 1969 or '70. It has funded about fifty assessments covering a wide range of physical, biological, social, electronic, and management technologies, as well as a large number of methodological development efforts. The NSF program is in my judgement largely responsible for sustaining and developing national and even international interest in TA; for advancing the state of the art and creating a body of shared learning. NSF sustained and encouraged a community of TA practitioners during the critical early years of TA development.

NSF had the advantage of a general mandate to support applied science relevant to national needs and problems, and the advantage of <u>not</u> having a specific technological or problem management mission as did other agencies. Therefore NSF was able to identify and address technological advances which cut across the responsibilities of several agencies or did not fall within the jurisdiction of any agency. Potential users of NSF assessments included a range of governmental and non-governmental decisionmakers including public interest groups. Therefore NSF was able to encourage the early identification of emerging technologies, the use of broadly exploratory techniques, and a general approach which was holistic, highly interdisciplinary and highly integrative in intent, if not always in outcome. Recently the NSF program has been putting greater emphasis on "policy relevance". In my opinion there is some danger that this emphasis may tend to downgrade the special advantage that NSF assessments have had and the special role that they have played.

To turn to the topic of information technology and telecommunications: in spite of the wide recognition that this cluster of new and rapidly developing technologies will almost certainly play a major - and possibly predominant - role in shaping the society of the future, there has been surprisingly little high quality impact assessment in this area, in the United States. (As an aside, I like to use the term "telematics" coined by Nora and Minc, to cover all of those technologies which record and store, manipulate, and communicate information.) Possibly the potential societal impacts of telematics are so dramatic and so pervasive that they can be addressed easily only at the theoretical or structural level, using concepts such as Daniel Bell's "post-industrial society" and Zbigniew Brzezinski's "Technotronic Age". More likely, the paucity of assessment results from the fact that no major Federal line agency has telematics development as its primary responsibility. Further, while there are a multitude of policy issues related to this technology, none has had the saliency, immediacy, and breadth of concern to become a major focus of political activity or to mobilize highly vocal interest groups, as do national concerns such as energy and environmental problems. Instead, the issues related to information technology tend to be relegated to administrative/regulatory processes, to the courts, and to minor legislative committees.

OTA has had a telecommunications assessment program for several years, however. Its major report is forthcoming in the near future, but until now there has been little public or Congressional visibility for this asssessment. A special national commission studied electronic funds transfer but gave relatively little attention to potential social impacts.

The National Science Foundation, however, has sponsored a number of assessments of telematics in the last few years. This is in fact a good example of NSF's ability, already noted, to address issues which other agencies have been unable or unwilling to address. Since Dr. Johnson, who has managed these studies for NSF, is participating in this conference, I need not comment further on these assessments. However I was Principal Investigator or a participant in several of these NSF assessments, and I would like to offer for your consideration several observations which I believe can help to guide the search for potential impacts of telematics.

It appears to me that telematics are in some ways the most challenging and most difficult topics for impact assessment. The most important impacts usually do not stem directly from the physical characteristics of the technology, although of course materials and energy demands and risks to health must be thoroughly investigated. The most important impacts however seem to be related to the capabilities offered by the technology and the way in which it will be used, and they are manifested in terms of changes in behaviour, institutional structures and functions, in efficiency and productivity, and in power relationships. These are much subtler, more complex, and more difficult to display than changes in the flow of dollars, materials, energy, or finished goods. Telematics manipulate, store, and transmit or receive symbols, and these symbols are the media through which all relationships within the society are established, sanctioned, controlled, promulgated, and propagated. These relationships of conflict, consensus, cooperation, integration, authority and obedience, and exchange of goods, services, and ideas are truly the structural-functional prerequisites of organized society. It is for this reason that telematic technologies are likely to have profound impacts.

I suggest that there are five further characteristics of telematics that make it nearly certain that each significant change in this technology will have important impacts. These characteristics then become useful maps for the search aimed at identifying these impacts. The five characteristics which I have in mind are the following:

o <u>These technologies allow operations, activities, and functions to be dispersed while control and guidance is centralized.</u> Thus the technologies allow or facilitate changes in the basic organizational structure of institutions and entire societies. (One can draw analogies with the function of mutations in physical evolution.) The developing political/economic ideology of "decentralization" is feasible in a complex society (whether or not it is desirable is another question) only because of the existing or potential capabilities of information technology. On the other hand, it was earlier advances in communications technology which to a large extent allowed the development of national cohesion and market integration in the United States, then a very large, thinly-populated, politically sundered developing nation, after 1864. In a different, purely physical sense, telematics allows human activities to be extended into locations where humans themselves cannot function or penetrate, for example, outer space.

o <u>They are networking technologies.</u> Telematics creates links between entities which were previously unconnected -- between geographical locations, between markets, between institutions, between data bases, between activities, and between theoretical constructs. In creating connections, they also may create interdependencies. The possibility of disruption of an established dependency is a vulnerability. Vulnerabilities evoke protective responses. Thus chains of direct and indirect changes, or impacts, are set in motion.

o <u>They change the way in which people, institutions, and societies budget their time.</u> Changes in the ways in which time must be used tends to have significant social and institutional impacts. By affecting the time budgets of individuals and families, television had important effects on family life, education, and competing leisure activities; by affecting the way in which organizations and managers budget time, computers have caused institutions to restructure activities, programs, and workforces, and to end some programs or activities and create others. Telematics has had and will have profound effects on the time that can be or must be allocated to many kinds of scientific and intellectual procedures, and has made possible some mathematical efforts which could not have been performed previously.

Thus telematics affects the efficiency and productivity of many other technologies and so affects innumerable choices between technological and social alternatives.

o <u>The alternative technologies for which information technologies can be substituted are often uniquely "human technologies."</u> Most new technologies substitute for an older technology, providing incremental improvement in effectiveness and efficiency. Those technologies which

directly replace human effort -- for example, the harnes-
sing of energy, the mechanization of agriculture, the
invention of printing -- have in the past had particularly dramatic societal impacts. To some extent information
technology potentially replaces the most uniquely human
expenditure of effort: the manipulation, disaggregation,
and recombining of data to produce new information. We
are barely in sight of the profound implications which
this may have for society.

Renate Mayntz

Social Science Research about the Consequences of Modern Information Technologies

I have been asked to talk about social science research on consequences of information technologies in particular and rather briefly. Information technology poses a special challenge to social science research, and at the same time confronts it with very specific and rather large problems. The basic reason for this has been roughly described, by implication, in what Mrs. Coates said before. Information technology is linked to one of the very elementary processes of human interaction and human behaviour, i.e. communication and the processing of information. From this it obviously follows that most social processes, institutions, or events have an information and communication aspect and are therefore liable to be affected by this particular technology. This means that more than other technological developments, information technologies pose problems and questions to be answered by social science research. By comparison, in the field of bio-technology the scope for social science research on particular impacts is much narrower.

The vast impact of developments in information technology also becomes evident if you consider that whatever analytical level the social scientist deals with, whether you take the individual, the organizational, or the societal (the system) level, there are relevant impacts of information technologies foreseeable. A typical example at the individual level is social research into the effects of the new communication media like videotext or viewdata on family life, individual leisure behaviour, and individual communication with various service institutions. At the organizational level, information technology impacts are studied not only in industrial enterprises but increasingly also in public sector organizations, where information technology also affects the relations between administration offices and clients. This indicates that the scope of the effects of this particular technology is much larger than the effects of previous developments in automation, which were closely

circumscribed to the industrial sector. The consequences of
information technologies on the societal level are pervasive
yet often diffuse. The one specific consequence that is
usually mentioned is the impact on employment. More diffuse
are possible effects on power relations in society, which
were also referred to in the Nora/Minc-Report. It is furthermore probable that there will be impacts on the mode of
social integration, the type of social networks in which
social processes work and social dynamics develop. But beyond such very general statements, not even the social scientist perceives very well the aggregate effect of these
various impacts.

This is where the problems come in. Since information technology involves basic processes of human behaviour and human
interaction, the effects are so manifold and so pervasive
that we are obviously faced with highly aggregate phenomena,
i.e. the addition of effects on many different levels, (individual, organizational and societal) and in many if not
all of the functional subsystems of society. Whether we take
the economy or the political sector, the health system or
the educational system, whether we take intermediary organizations for interest representation and political opinion
formation, there is no functional area in society which is
not potentially affected by changes in information technologies. But these changes are interdependent, so that where-
ever we start, we are dealing with the aggregate effects of
very complex interactions. This is what makes the problem so
difficult to cope with, intellectually and in terms of research technology for the social sciences. How does social
science face up to this particular challenge?

Of course it will not be possible to give a pervasive and
global survey referring to different countries. The focus of
my remarks is on the German Federal Republic. There are two
aspects which should be taken into account: how does the

scientific community, especially the social sciences, react to this challenge, and to what extent have the responsible political institutions perceived and reacted to this particular aspect of information technology development, for instance by starting specific social science programs to assess the relevant impacts. These two questions should be kept apart.

Let me start with the first aspect, the spontaneous reaction of the social science community. In Germany we do have particular difficulties with research not only on information technology, but on all kinds of technology: for what reasons ever, social scientists do not like very much to get deeply involved in questions of technological development. I will not go into this in detail, but education has surely something to do with it. Compared with countries like Britain, our German educational system does not provide us with a significant number of persons who in the course of their academic training, starting either from the social sciences or from engineering etc., have received sufficient knowledge from the other, complementary side. We have available very few researchers trained in two disciplines and therefore commanding the requisite knowledge for approaching this kind of social-impact-of-technology research.

If you look at existing research, it has a special focus in this particular field, i.e. technology and work. "Work" is here perceived mainly as work in industry, the secondary sector. The tertiary sector is coming up slowly, but it is still very much second in line. The questions dealt with in research are mainly those which industrial sociology has traditionally approached, i.e. work and work satisfaction, the impact of technology on the content of work. The perspective of industrial sociology with its focus on the individual work place and the individual worker is now applied also to service industries in the tertiary sector and very slowly also to public administration. In my opinion this traditional way of analysing the problem is rather insufficient to deal with the specific nature of information technology. To summarize: the general level of interest is too low, and the focus is not where from a normative point it should be, starting from the nature of the problem that is actually posed.

If you ask to what extent the major German research funding organizations are recognizing this deficiency and sponsoring integrated research programs in the particular area, the answer is so far negative. The Volkswagen Foundation, the one major private research funding agency, has no program in this particular area and no program under which projects of this sort could easily be categorized. The German counterpart of the National Science Foundation, the Deutsche Forschungsgemeinschaft, has very recently started to develop a special program on technology and society, which is already now, before it ever gets off the ground, in danger of being dominated by the traditional industrial sociology approach.

Turning to the research sponsorship by government agencies, we can observe that in contrast to such countries as France (vid. the Nora/Minc-Report), but also in contrast to a small country like Austria, the German Federal Government has not started a specific major initiative to sponsor a social science investigation in this field. The Nora/Minc-Report of course is not a social science report in the narrow sense, but it is a major analysis of the societal effects and expected impacts. We do not have a German counterpart to this. Nor do we have a German counterpart to the Austrian study, which is not yet published. The Austrian initiative started a few years ago when Christopher Freeman gave a lecture on the likely effects of microelectronics on the labour force etc., and a number of officials from the Austrian Ministry of Science and Research who attended the lecture were shocked by the perspective that opened before them and started an initiative to get an assessment of what this development might mean to the Austrian economy and society. The research program then started asking some rather typical questions. They wanted to have a technological forecast, they wanted to have the macroeconomic aspect covered, but this is not where the program stopped; in fact, heavy emphasis was also put on the social aspects and consequences and on possible socioeconomic alternatives to the apparently spontaneous forces of development.

In Germany this kind of official reaction has not been observed. If we look more in detail at the social science research sponsored by our Ministry of Research and Technology, we can briefly see the following pattern emerge. Talking now not only about information technology but technological development in general, the German government and this Ministry in particular has gone through a series of phases in relation to promoting technological R & D. The first impulse in post-war Germany obviously was to catch up with technological development elsewhere. The second phase was dominated by the effort to close the perceived technological gap developing between Europe, and Germany in particular, on one hand and the United States on the other hand. Japan at that time was not visible as a new threat. Then in a third phase came the recognition, starting when the so-called economic miracle was waning, that there exists a close link between technological and economic development, stimulating the attempt to use technology policy and research on technology as an instrument for ultimately economic goals. Today this is still the dominant perspective, and it is also the dominant perspective in the research on information technology sponsored by the Ministry. Recently, however, acceptance problems in the area of nuclear energy have led to the insight that technological innovations in all fields might run into acceptance problems and that this might ultimately have political consequences. This is presently leading to a certain reorientation, foremost at the level of explicit research policy, though not yet very pronounced at the level of actual research funding. There is a recent sociological study undertaken by the science research unit at the University of Bielefeld which brings out this point. The analysis refers particularly to the field of information technology and the way the Federal Ministry of Research and Technology is dealing with it. The major results in this analysis are the following. There are a number of programs where, especially in very recent years, on the programmatic level attention is paid to social, political, and cultural effects of information technology. As a secondary focus of interest this occurs in several research programs, but it is not the primary goal of any one program so far. Looking at research funding, we see that money goes first into research on the technical development per se, i.e. is sponsorship of technological innovation. Second in line is research on economic effects, mainly macroeconomic effects, including employment. Together this accounts for something like 75% or 80% of the studies analysed over several years. The number of projects involving social science aspects is relatively small, and the major focus is again in the field of work organizations. This means that of the three analytical levels here distinguished, the social science research sponsored by the Ministry involving information technologies focuses on the organizational level. It is seen that on the societal level there are enormous problems ahead, but they are still very diffuse and therefore it seems even difficult to formulate precise research questions on the macro-level.

Without extending this survey (though some initiatives by other ministries or at the Länder level might be mentioned), enough has been said to give a brief impression of the research scene and to show that in Germany at this time there is still a significant discrepancy between the recognized

challenge which the impact of developments in information
technology poses to social science (and to society) on the
one hand and the actual research, whether government sponsored or coming spontaneously from the scientific community,
on the other hand.

Bernd-Peter Lange, Jürgen Reese

Impact Research and Research Policy
An Analytical Framework

1. Stating the problem

Unintended and unexpected impacts of technology make experimental research and development a thrilling part of human being. Often they turn out to be very useful for a society, but many times they do not. Thus, the innovating scientist, engeneer, manager or politician tries to control the pay off of his decisions on technological developments, and he looks for alternatives if it seems necessary to him. So far technologies develop within constraints being set by more or less powerful organizations and markets.

Different from this feature is the development of technologies which allow an insight in their impacts as late as their implementation has reached a point of no return. At least two types of technologies imply the point of no return risk:

a) Small sized technics with wholesale application mainly on the custumer's level, e.g. Television and automobils. Their impacts are directly connected either with their mass production and hence result from a complex socio-technical infrastructure with slow depreciation and change, or with their mass consumption or use and the succeeding change of consumer's attitudes and burdens.

b) Very large sized technics with a demand for an extended planning and construction period, e.g. military airplanes and nuclear power plants. Their impacts seem incalculable until very large sums of money have been invested.

Generally speaking a technology becomes irreversible when its production and distribution have created a large sized organization, and when many people directly or indirectly live from it.

Both types of technics set up the same dilemma: we can reach their benefits only at the risk of negative impacts, and the net outcome can be even worse than the situation was before the use of the technic. This dilemma is a challenge to modern industrial societies. It is also the starting point of our analysis here. Can we hope to cope with it by developing and using more sophisticated methods of impact prognosis? Or do we have to organize the process of development and implementation of new technologies in a different way so that the point of no return is put forward?

2. The rational approach

It is a matter of fact that serious efforts to predict with scientific methods possible impacts of new technologies can be traced back for only about 15 years. Obviously these attempts focus on large sized technics. They have been stimulated and in some cases also institutionalized by organizations in connection with R&D policies, mostly by political organizations. This indicates the increasing political costs of the fiscal support to the development of large sized technics. People feel more and more the environmental threat which can emanate from them. Often they appeal to the political organizations. Thus, the analysis of social and environmental impacts as well as the analysis of the acceptance of a large sized technology has to be interpreted as a reaction on menacing losses of mass loyalty. The term technology assessment (TA) is closely conneceted with these circumstances.

From a strict methodological standpoint assessing technology as a risk avoiding or risk reducing strategy presupposes a list of conditions:

a) the technology must be separate so that it can be clearly
   defined,
b) information about the internal structure of the technology must be exhaustive (adaptability, variability
   of use),

c) there has to exist a reliable causal theory about the
   economic and societal implementation process of the
   technology,

d) there has to be a value order for judgements on the
   impacts. The order has to be explicit, consistent, and
   there has to be agreement on it,

e) the analytical process beginning with the definition
   of the technology and ending with recommendations has
   to have time enough before the point of no return in
   the technological development is reached,

f) since different actors have different interests there
   has to be a centralized power structure to effectively
   draw conclusions.

In nearly all cases of relevant technology assessment many
of these conditions are not existent. Therefore, the involved analysts use substitutes and they reduce their
claims. Both strategies are convenient for writing a report
but at the same time they diminish the conclusive force.
Within a system with many decision makers and contradictory
interests they make the report ineffective. The argument
is not principally directed against the use of social sience
methods for forecasting and assessing technologies. It refers only on the exchange of ressources between the political institutions and the consulting scientist. For clari-
fication we will point out some dangers of technology
assessment as it is used in practice.

3. Shortcomings of the rational approach

Technology assessment is thoroughly a consulting activity: As a type of analysis it derives from a political demand. Single analyses are regularly charged by political organizations and ordered for special purposes in decision-making contexts. These facts do not exclude an intrinsic motivation of the analyst, neither his use of scientific methods. But they imply some restrictions which possibly cannot be accepted.

- Taking the initiative for technology assessment political organizations can exclude unwelcome studies, and if they decide to order a study they can pick out researchers whose paradigms fit into the organizational demands. Thus, on the individual level no one is constrained, but on the systems level technology assessment has a tendency to confirm institutional expectations. (We stress the so-called non decision argument here.)

- The scope of time for technology assessment is regularly limited because of acute political needs. As a consequence the assessments have also a very limited theoretical scope. This weakens their complexity and their value for prognoses. Perhaps more detrimental is the fact that many studies are not comparable and do not allow theoretical generalizations. As a consequence there is no cumulating effect for methodology and theory.

- Less theoretical but more pragmatic intentions of analysts should strengthen their interest in knowledge about the implementation and political effects of their assessments. Perhaps in doing so they could improve their efficacy, otherwise they would at least contribute to political theory. But unfortunately the orderer of technology assessment is not interested in information of that kind at all. Therefore he will not pay for it.

- Technology assessment will merely be ordered for small sized technics because these technics usually do not extensively depend on political support. It is true that they develop and diffuse within politcal rules (laws, technical norms, construction regulations and so on), but on the other hand the remaining scope is still very wide. Depending on that fact politicians will not feel responsible for these technics and their impacts. (A good example is the speed limit. Nobody insists on the political responsiveness for accident rates on roads.)

- The inescapable value judgements of technology assessments result in the political demand for balanced value judgements. There is no doubt that the center of balance will usually be defined by the orderer of the assessment.

- Technology assessments are decision-making oriented. They presuppose a general political influence and a scope of R&D policy which do not exist in many cases. One might argue that inefficiency would not harm, but as a matter of fact this proceeding strengthens the false doctrine of omnipotent political institutions instead of the more correct assumption that a technology is the result of extremely fragmental and sequential decision-making processes.

The catalogue shows the socio-political framework in which technology assessment develops as a practice. The framework gives evidence that technology assessment offers neither the whole potential of analysis nor the range of knowledge which we need so badly to cope with the point of no return problem in technological developments. Therefore the critique turns primarily against the practice or, let us say, against the technology assessment policy. Obviously science about technology must not depend on ephemeral demands of political organizations. In addition, the use of the rational approach neglects indispensible principles of scientific reasoning, because it concedes the disjoining of methods and purposes. It is mainly this reason which leads to the separation of technology assessment and an impact analysis using the socio-technical approach.

4. The socio-technical approach

Impact research or impact analysis has to be appropriate to the high complexity of impact contexts. According to this imperative we do not only have to ask: What kinds of technics do have what kind of impacts, but we have also to ask: Who develops technology with what interests? (At present we face dramatic examples of interconnected impacts and interests in West Germany, where the labour unions have to make up their mind about the use of nuclear energy as well as about the extensive use of robots and computers.)

Let us elaborate the argument with two examples:

- A hammer is a very useful technical instrument, but in use it makes noise. The noise is reasonable unless we use the hammer for instance at night or during a string quartet.

- A moped makes many miles per gallon and thus it seems to offer an economic transport. But if it is used by teenagers to drive ten times around the same block it animates obviously to energy waste.

As we can see social norms and attitudes determine the impacts of technics. But in as many cases the incentives stem from different reasons, as it can be shown with this example:

- A manager decides to computerize the stock-keeping with the saving up effect of ten employees. He increases the productivity and improves the statement of his firm.

In this case the background of technical use is an organized interest since the manager is paid for the described behaviour.

There is no doubt that the impacts of a technic depend heavily on the social context of its use. As a consequence we cannot seriously study the impacts of technologies without paying attention to the social dynamic of its development, use, and current adjustment. Even less successful will be an attempt to predict future impacts if the causal complexity is cut down. Impact research implies the explicit effort in the analysis of attitudes and interests. As to the question which interests and attitudes will prove as dominating the forecasting of impacts presupposes also an analysis of the structure of societal power. Having a look on Table 1 the argument will be explained in a more systematic way.

The invention and development of a new technology usually takes place in an R&D firm or devision. Of all theoretically existent options there will be invented and developed only a selection. Very little is known about the underlying selection principles, if there are any. But the interests, consciousness, values, and capabilities of owners, managers, and engineers obviously play an important role in the selection process.

Suppose the outcome of that process is a <u>basic technology</u> like mechanics, pneumatics, hydraulics, semiconductor technic, data processing. Basic technologies (or simply tech-

T A B L E   1

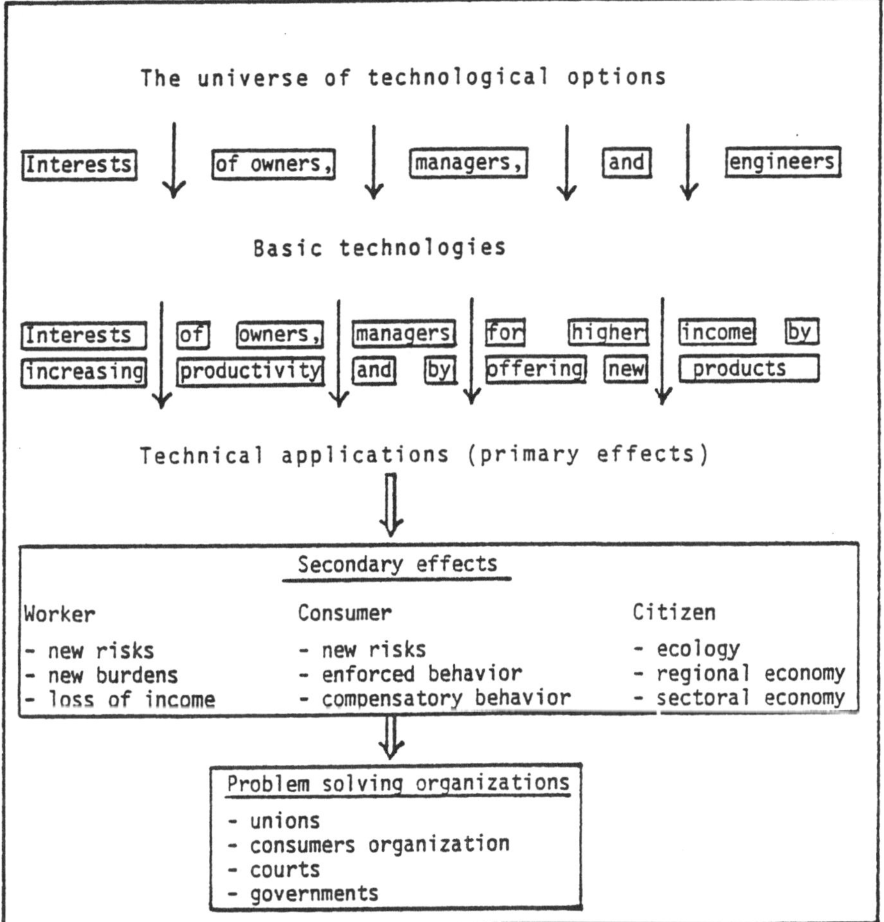

nologies) can be defined as a distinct set of knowledge. This knowledge includes natural laws, logical constructions, and mechanical treatments. Then, the basic technology has to be transformed into a tool before it can be efficiently used. Such a tool usually combines different basic technologies to a <u>technical application</u>.

Different from a basic technology a technical application is directed to special purposes. Simple tools like a saw or a knife have a wide range of applications, but even they are already characterized by their purpose. Complex tools like a computer program or an airplane have a less wide range of applications and purposes. They are determined by buyers interests. In the production sector that means mainly the interest in higher productivity, whereas in the consumption sector the interests are generally directed to new, cheaper, and better products. For our argument it is important to see here that the first interest articulation, which is decisive for the choice of a technical application, comes from the producer ("primary effects").

In the next step the technical application has a more or less wide range of impacts:

- a new production technic leads to a reorganization. It affects the division of labour, the labour skills and the social and ecological environment at the work place. There can be an increase of burdens and risks for employees and a partial or total loss of income.

- On the consumption side a new technical good can create new risks and it can induce a behavioral change.

In addition a new technology can also have more or less strong impacts on the ecology and on the regional and sectoral economy. All these impacts may be summarized as "secondary effects".

Since the primary effects set the standard for the development as well as for the application of a technic they will usually be achieved. Positive evaluated secondary effects will be accepted as a welcome side effect. But negative effects (more precisely negative net effects) can lead to a whole range of reactions with increasing strength:

- individual suppression
- sublimation by individual compensation
- individual flight
- individual protest
- collective protest
- strike, respectively change of voting

According to the conflict power there are different institutionalized ways for mediation, arbitration and ad-
judication im modern societies (contracts between shop
stewards/unions and employers, legislatures, and courts).
Taken together they set legal and technical constraints
for the use of technics. Thus, the third step of a technical application can be its prohibition, certain restraints
to its use of directions for its modification.

The argument points out that the prove of a technical
application depends not only on the pure technical effectiveness but also on its adaptation to individual and
societal needs. In this sense a real proved technical
application is a socio-technical system.

Having this in mind the first mentioned objection against
technology assessment will become somewhat clearer. The
final definition of a technic which is to be assessed is
possible only at the cost of neglecting its evolutionary
dimension. Thus, the assessment is focussed on the most
crucial point of prediction, i.e. on the sociological and
psychological compatibility of a not yet existing technic.

On the background of an evolutionary concept the competing
socio-technical approach of impact research comes to different starting points. To begin with the possible negative
impacts of a technical application the afflicted persons

or groups have to be informed about it at a very early stage. They can make up their mind with consequences of the technic before it is used. The role of the scientist is threefold: a) He has to find out the possibly afflicted groups. b) He has to organize their learning about the technic and their interest articulation. c) He has to manage conflicting interests in terms of forms of participation. This element of impact research is very much related to action research.

The second task of impact research follows from the need for political interventions. They are necessary especially in the field of highly developed technical infrastructures like electrical power provision, airport systems, and telephone communication. This kind of impact research, which comes methodologically very close to technology assessment, is legitimated by the cumulative effects of such technics. Since these effects may be relatively neglectable from the standpoint of every affected person and organization, they sum up to national relevant disadvantages. If, for instance, the public bureaucracy plans the implementation of a complex computer system for its own use this should not be an object to impact research of the second but of the first type.

Government interventions are disputed because of their effectiveness. Therefore a public attempt to influence the use of new technics needs occasional evaluations with conclusions for the range and instruments of further intervening activities. This is the instrumental oriented impact research.

As we have shown above the main interest in the development of technics is an increase of productivity and income (new products). Thus, already the selection criteria within the technical development determine the impact research to play a reactive and restrictive role, whenever it finds negative social or ecological effects of a technical application. On this background we should ask wether it is possible to actively develop basic technologies to new applications primarily in favour of the solutions of social or ecological problems. In this case one should start with the analysis of social problems and then search into the possible help by special technical applications. This kind of an inverted causality of technical development can be called social technology. Its starting point is so to speak the intended impact instead of the unintended impact.

All these forms of impact research are systematically linked by the structural analysis of socio-technical systems. None of them can cope with the bias of the predominating selection processes alone. They all belong together and have to be set in operation, if the whole benefitial power of technology shall be developed with as little risk as possible. In the last part of our paper we will elaborate this approach for the field of information technology. This can be done only in a very rough way here. More precise work is listed at the end of the paper. Table 2 shows a rough comparison between the two explained approaches.

5. Impact research in the field of information technology

a) Analytical impact research

As we have pointed out the timeliness of analytical impact research is important because the use of newly developed technics can hardly be directed effectively, once they have led to high capital investment for

T A B L E   2

The main differences between the rational
and the socio-technical approach

Analytical approaches

Criteria	rational (Technology assessment)	socio-technical (Impact research)
Initiative	Government	Researchers
Address	Government	Primarily other Researchers and interested groups
Communication	Possibly confidential	Public
Interests	Information support to government decision making	Depends on the researcher.
Decision	yes or no	modifications
Selectivities:		
- technologies	large sized technics	all technics
- values	dominating interests	plurality of values and interests
- methods	reliability oriented	validity oriented
Basic perspective (paradigma)	linear causality of technic → society	mutual causality technic ↔ society
Methodology	single level approach	multiple level approach

their development and use, and have brought about a social organization that "lives of them". Accordingly, socially responsible impact research must dare to anticipate possibly dubious or even dangerous developments, despite possessing an inadequate state of knowledge. Nevertheless the impact researcher who forges ahead in analytic anticipation of social developments in the future has to recognize his responsibility for an empirical and theoretical justification of his theses and must strive to achieve it. This is extremly important as we are aware that a mere linear extension of existing trends does not take into account the qualitative breaks in the developments of the applications of technologies. So, the experiences in a pilot project only give a restricted answer to the question for social impact of the application of a wide spread technology.

Individual applications of information technology will alter immensely entire sectors of economy during the next decade. This seems true particularly for office automation in the service sector, for the applications of electronic fund transfer in the banking sector and for the use of robots in the industrial sector. Individual analysis of these sectors appears, therefore, most necessary. Just because the spread of information technics cannot be stopped in these sectors, changes of jobs conditions, changes of needed qualifications and changes of social organizations that will result purely from strategy of rationalization require exhaustive analysis. In this manner, impact research can create important requisites to help avoiding serious consequences for employees by suitable legal and organizational means, when analytic, pragmatic and instrumental impact research go together.

Another field of widespread applications of information
technics are the 'new media' as cabletelevision, viewdata and teletex. It should be one of the tasks of
impact research to analyse - at least in a broadbrash
fashion - on the one hand the marketing chances and,
thereby, also the probable marketing ways of new media
in the hands of privat enterprise owner/operators and
on the other hand the long range impacts of television,
sponsored by commercials on the socialization of our
youth, on the communication in the family and on the
social structure in one dimension determined by knowledge. Then the current discussion in Germany on the
organization of mass media would be more oriented to
facts than to vested interests.

One of the graver misgivings, tied closely to the drift
towards an information society, refers to the mounting
social control of the individual. True, the problem
is quite current in discussions of safe-guarding data,
but as a rule, it has been viewed in too narrow a context and there also have not been researches so far in
the social context. On the one hand the task here
consists of obtaining a clearer picture of the unavoid-
able governmental data requirements needed for planning
and carrying out of laws. On the other hand it consists
of producing analyses of those changes in the quality
of life and behaviour of the individual resulting from
such controls. In this field especially pluralistic
impact research and a controversial discussion of social
aims is very much needed.

The results of these individual impact researches have
to be combined in broader structural analyses. In this
case a better understanding of the dynamism, which information technology injects into modern society, could
be brought forth. An important prerequisite for under-

standing this dynamism is, first of all, an as exact analysis as is possible of the change in economic structure, which should also include the growing international interlocking of business relations. Therefore, the different individual results of specific impact research have to be related to an analysis of the changing economic system. A second step in the structural approach is the analysis of the changing political system. Applications of information technics in the field of social policy and in the field of mass media will influence the further development of democracy.

Stress and pressures upon man at work and at leisure have been researched many times. Also, the specific problems of individual applications of technics lead time and again to projects which examine the interrelation between man, technical science, organization of labor or family. Such research, devoted to individual uses of technics, certainly suffices no longer when the individual has to suffer from changes in various lifespheres simultaneously, as happens due to the "information technological revolution". Impact research in a third step of structural approach must, therefore, try especially to analyse the cumulative effects of information technology upon the individual while on the job, in the political sphere and when at leisure. It must pass from the partial, role-oriented kind of analysis to a more integral view. A special task for analysis of the social system lies in elaborating the gradual blurring of the borderlines between labor and reproduction. In any case analytic impact research has to be oriented to the future and has to discuss the standards of evaluation in conflicts of interests.

b) <u>Pragmatic impact research</u>

The general task of pragmatic impact research is to
establish and maintain communication between the deve-
lopers of technology (engineers, informatics specialists,
mathematicians, and the industries concerned) and those
who become affected by the employment of such technics.
Efforts of developing humane technics are not new.
Rather, there is a large number of technics that show
the influence of the psychologist or ergonomics expert.
To include medical or labor science aspects in the
development of technology is indeed no problem as long
as it is merely a matter of appropriate forms and colors
of design. Causal attribution of back troubles, eye
diseases, and headaches can be made relatively reliable
by experimental test use of prototypes, resulting in
correspondingly cogent arguments of such auxiliary
sciences in a technical development. After all, form
and color designs are relatively easily changed without
interfering with function of the equipment.

Considerably more difficult is the solution of the
problem in the case of complex information and communication systems. They lead increasingly to a complete
reorganization of the work operation and, in future very
likely, of the private life with consequences, some of
which will not be recognized as being due to technics
in the most exact analyses. Here, humane application of
technics can only mean that wherever those affected by
handling the technics are unable to decide autonomously
on how to use it they are assured of adequate consideration of their needs and interests.

Forms of pragmatic or participatory impact research
have to be used wherever more complex technics are to
be implemented within organizations like private firms

or public bureaucracies. Since the initial hypotheses
of that research are the changing division of labour,
the changing skills, the changing burdens, the most
important technological applications are complex computerized information systems, office automation, and
robot technics.

c) <u>Instrumental impact research</u>

Analytical and pragmatic impact research, no matter how
effective they may become, cannot themselves solve most
of the problems enumerated. Such research will have to
receive assistance in the form of governmental policy
and of appropriate legislative measures, especially
where market forces compel business and managerial decisions into the general trend of rationalizing for the
sake of efficiency. In the same time instruments used
by the trade unions influence the development of information technologies. Which instruments will prove
finally to be more suitable will depend on individual
situations of problems and interests.

In West Germany, as everywhere internationally, various
governmental interventions are used without any particular exact analyses commensurate with the goals of
such intervention being undertaken. So-called evaluation
research, which is slowly to deal with such questions
in other spheres of governmental policy, has not yet
recognized the instruments with which government manages
problems of the information society for what they surely
are: A rich field for analysis - fertile above all, because constructive contributions are still much in demand
in this period of widespread helplessness.

Even today, testimony on the use of instruments can go
a step further in cases where it is not so much a

question of legal or organizational intervention by the government – i.e. of precepts and prohibitions – but, rather, a matter of governmental investments and public incentives. This applies especially to sponsorship of research. Such sponsorship has tried to support the domestic information technological industry with considerable sums in pursuit of the generally uncontested goal of "modernizing the economy". As it becomes now increasingly clear, an unchanged continuation of this policy would lead not only to an intensification of the positive effects, caused by information technology in the German Federal Republic, but also to an exacerbation of the negative ones. The kind of problems that become intensified through such sponsorship of research gives rise to the expectation that in the intermediate or farther future the government itself must bear responsibility for the consequences – primarily in the form of additional fiscal burdens caused by an increased social affairs budget.

In consequence of such results of instrumental impact research there has to be a better coordination of different instruments, influencing the development of information technology. As in the other fields of impact research, social science can make proposals in a controversial discussion on adequate instruments. It is to the politicians to decide and to bear the responsibility for the main directions of social change.

d) <u>Social impact research</u>

Social problems are at most manifestations of a broad range of causes, and often they mark the endpoint of a history so that the real causes are covered or even withdrawn from todays manipulation. Class conflicts and many territorial conflicts are good examples for social problems, the history of which is gone beyond the point of peaceful resolutions. Information technology could help here only as part of weapons. But even less virulent social problems are neither caused by lacking information and communication nor can they be mitigated by an improvement of those functions. Social impact research has as well to elaborate very carefully the specific social potential of information technology as it has to select social problems which could at least partially be resolved by special applications of information technology.

According to a recently concluded study on social information technology we differentiate four groups of possible positive impacts of information technology within the context of social problems:

- information systems for individual use by the "client",
- information systems for professional problem solvers (e.g. social workers),
- matching systems which help to arrange mutual help on the grassroot level,
- context changing systems which improve the life conditions directly (e.g. cable TV for old people, protheses).

Generally speaking there are many groups in modern societies, which suffer from insulation, loneliness, special risks or diseases. Many of them could be helped with one or a set of these technics. But there is a precondition: The already existing technical systems cannot be used unless they are modified according to the special needs of the group. Often complete new applications will have to be developed.

Before this can be done the researcher has to identify
the social problem, to define the specific information,
communication, and context problem and he has to analyze
the specific behavior of people within the group so
that he can define the conditions for the later acceptance of the technic.

Literature

H. Kubicek, Interessenberücksichtigung beim Technikeinsatz im Büro- und Verwaltungsbereich, Berichte der Gesellschaft für Mathematik und Datenverarbeitung Nr. 125, München 1979.

B.-P. Lange et al., Chancen der informationstechnologischen Entwicklung. Zur staatlichen Förderung einer sozialen Informationstechnologie, Frankfurt a.M. 1982.

H. Paschen et al., Technology Assessment: Technologiefolgenabschätzung, Frankfurt 1978.

J. Reese et al., Gefahren der informationstechnologischen Entwicklung, Frankfurt a.M. 1979.

J. Reese, Social Policies and Technical Options, in: Information Society: for richer, for poorer, ed. by N. Bjørn-Andersen et al., Amsterdam 1982.

G. Ropohl et al., Maßstäbe der Technikbewertung, ed. by Verein Deutscher Ingenieure, Düsseldorf 1978.

Practicability, Applicability, and Benefits of Research on Impacts

-The Story Behind the Scenery -

The lack of a single, generally accepted set of concepts and the existence of a broad variety of objectives, functions, and philosophies also express the practical problems of research on technological impacts. On the one hand the ideals call for highly ambitious research, on the other hand research practice cannot meet this challenge, as some retrospective analyses of impact studies have demonstrated.

So far a convincing solution to this problem has not become apparent. Research is built on compromises. To meet constraints of economics and time, the level of ambition is often lowered and our attention is focussed on those aspects of the problems where the technological risks seem most pressing.

One way to cope with this dilemma is doing research on research. An assessment of methodological weaknesses could lead to new approaches or methods to overcome these deficiencies.

In the second session of the symposium the reality of technological assessment was inquired. The papers presented here showed current limitations concerning the practicability, applicability and benefits of impact research.

Peter Mertens demonstrated with "The NSI Project" the problem of prognoses. His analyses of the actual effects of information technologies did not support assumptions often mentioned in this context. G. Patrick Johnson gave a "Review of Selected Technology Assessment Studies of Information Technologies in the United States of America". In his presentation he clarified problematic issues related to an information society and pointed out the respective policy issues for which the impact studies can or have been helpful. Ida R. Hoos accentuated in her contribution "Pitfalls of Current Methodologies of Technology Assessment - Can We

Avoid the Negative Effects of Information Technology Assessment" the systemic and methodological impossibility of carrying out technology assessment which provides any hope of escaping the negative effects of an information society.

The inadequacy of research methods is a heavily debated issue in impact research as we do not have a specific set of assessment methods. Research methods come from many disciplines, and the restrictions observed in their traditional field of application are also valid for technological assessments. New methods which cope with the very characteristics of impact research still need to be developed.

After several years of experience with impact research there cannot be clearly stated any preference for certain methods. It is first and foremost the subject to be assessed which determines the appropriate methods. Accordingly, with every new assessment task the researcher will have to go through the selection problem again. Previous experience is of course a help in selecting methodologies but should also be viewed with some caution because of the unique nature of each project.

In order to get a better understanding of expected changes and to recognize more complex relationships, structural models, highly aggregated simulation models, and scenario techniques have been applied with some success. But even if these "very scientific" methods seem to have produced convincing results we must be aware that the attitudes of the researcher to a high degree color the results. With the choice of the research team, the perspective and research paradigm is normally decided and the results are therefore already predetermined and predictable in a certain way.

One way to solve this dilemma is to charge two or more teams using different perspectives with the same assessment task.

The differences in the results would then provide clarifica-
tion on how different attitudes influence the outcomes and
would perhaps provide the decision maker with diverse alternative to choose from.

Projects which involve a multitude of people over periods of
several years produce additional problems. Often the work
intensity of each individual varies because the participants
are occupied with other work too. This interferes with the
research task and lowers the quality of the output. A more
preferable approach would be to divide the work into periods
of very intensive and undisturbed teamwork, maybe in a
secluded place, alternating with periods of more extensive
work including "data gathering" functions.

As stated earlier, one of the most important functions of
technology assessment is its translation and information
function. But the transfer of scientific results into practical usable results is often a problem. Politicians and the
public need to understand the research results. Research
reports written only to be understood by professionals
within the research field in question must be translated and
presented in a form more intelligible for non-professionals.
The National Science Foundation conducting some experiments
in order to improve this situation. They asked a group of
people to read a report, to check the important information
in the paper, to identify to whom it could be important and
why, and so on. These responses were used to produce a
"Readers Digest" version of the report. Even though the
experiments did not prove to be as successfull as desired,
the example illustrates a positive step and a growing
consciousness of the problem of producing more understandable presentations of research results.

Knowing about the limits of validity of findings, technology
assessment can be a useful and valuable tool in understanding the anxieties and potential hazards of new tech-

nological developments. Such criticism contributes to an increasing sensitivity about our responsibility to the future. For many years business firms have understood that short-term thinking endangers long run success. Technology assessment can help to increase the consciousness in society that we need strategic and long-term planning in order to cope with technological developments.

In its current state of development we cannot always assume that impact research will produce completely new information. But it can collect dispersed existing information in a systematic way and disclose new aspects.

E.g., intensive occupation with alternative perspectives of technological developments might help identifying critical crossroads where decisions have to be made in order to prevent undesired effects and to establish in time the preconditions and the environment for positive developments.

The occurence of technological impacts is dependent on a great number of factors, technical factors as well as social or economic factors. Societal areas which to-day are not seen at all to be related to a particular technology may suddenly change and then prove to be sensitive to technology applications. Because of these non-apparant, indirect relationships a positive cost-benefit of a technology application may turn into a negative cost-benefit for the society at large or for certain groups in society. Technology assessment might discover such relationships.

In this way technology assessment may considerably contribute towards the improvement of the political decision base.

Peter Mertens

The NSI Project

1. Goal

When analyzing the publications dealing with assessment of information technology and computer-assisted information systems in Germany we got the impression that most of them were written from a rather pessimistic point of view and that there was a considerable lack of empirical foundation.

So we started the NSI project, where NSI stands for "Nutzen und Schaden der Informationsverarbeitung" which might be translated to positive and negative impacts of information technology. The goal of the project was to provide for some more empirical evidence, and we wanted not only to look for the bad news but for the good news too.

2. Approach

As far as we see, there are four possible approaches to gain some empirical results concerning the effects of information technology:

1. In-depth case studies
2. A series of semi-structured interviews
3. Questionnaires
4. Literature analysis

We decided to select no. 2 and 4 from this catalogue both on a rather large scale.

The reasons for this selection were among others that, when performing case studies, you need a big portion of your research budget to get evidence on very few cases so that - with a given budget - you can draw only a very little sample. So you would have many difficulties in generalizing the results. Moreover you would have to pay attention to the

Hawthorne effects. As far as questionnaires are considered, my opinion is that the world is rather muddy by the many questionnaires sent out by sociologists and other researchers so that you can hardly expect to get good results. Moreover there is one research study on the matter based on questionnaires which was done by my colleague Eduard Gaugler from the Mannheim University.

First of all we collected approximately 1800 reports on the implementation of information systems. We took these reports from edp periodicals, from congress proceedings, from union publications etc., the only rule of the game being that nothing would be eliminated, wherever it came from, provided it was published after 1970 in English or German language. We made structured abstracts from all these reports using descriptors from a catalogue of 350. Then we stored the items in a simple data base. So we can select and retrieve the material using different combinations of descriptors, assemble it in different ways and tabulate simple statistics.

We call this part of our analysis the secondary analysis. One type of usage was to evolve some thesis for our primary analysis which consisted of 51 interviews in 39 organizations. 38 interviews were done with managers from the edp departments and 13 interviews with the shop stewards. 80 persons took part in these interviews. Our original design provided for interviews with one edp manager and one shop steward on the implementation of the same information system in the same organization, but unfortunately this design could not be realized because of several reasons. As we had more managers than labour representatives in our sample for certain analysis we tried to compensate for this drawback just by weighting the answers of the shop stewards three times. That seems to be a very simple but fair method.

When selecting the firms we tried to get a mix of industries such as production, trade, etc. Besides production we have a second main field in banking and assurance because in these industries there is a high ratio between display terminals and employees and because we have to expect a considerable rise in productivity by new information technology.

Another goal was to visit firms in different geografic areas.

The interviews were structured to a degree of about 80% and the answers were statistically analyzed using our method base system SAMBA which is a special version of SPSS.

3. <u>Some results</u>

The results are not yet published. Let's make a list of some results of our primary research:

1. Considering the reasons why new information systems are implemented, disposition and planning problems rank highest. The second reason is improvement of the service to the customers. It seems that the new information systems are used to come back to a certain individualization of the customer relationships whereas the last generation of batch processing systems helped to make mass data processing more effective.

2. The rise of labour costs was the third reason for the implementation of information systems, and 80% of the visited firms could diminish these costs.

3. Problems with the employees such as difficulties to hire, fluctuation, absentism ranked very low as a reason to implement computerized systems. This finding does not go

together with the assumption that the firms want to replace unreliable people by more reliable automata.

4. One of the highest ranking advantages of modern information systems in production lies in lowering the inven-
tories without impairing the service level.

5. The most cited negative effect of information systems is
that the firm becomes heavily dependent on the performance of the computer.

6. In the last years, more and more new systems are promoted
by the operational departments of the firm such as production, finance etc. whereas at earlier times the edp
people were the main promoters and had a lot of problems
to sell their ideas within the organization. In many firms
there are many applications of the line managers for new
information systems. This seems to be an indicator that
now many managers have recognized the advantages of edp.

7. In approximately one third of our cases the employees
participated in the implementation process, in another
third they were asked for advice during this process.

8. In one half of the cases there were some difficulties
with participating groups such as workers, shop stewards,
manufacturer of the computer or line managers, but mostly
the complaints were not aggrevating and the problems
could be solved by something like a round table discussion; only in few cases more formal letters were written
or other written documents on the problem were produced.

9. In about one half of our cases the number of the workplaces was reduced as a consequence of the implementation.
In 78% of the cases this reduction was carried out by the
so-called natural fluctuation and by transfer of the

workers to other jobs in the same firm. Only in 8% employees were fired.

10. We found a significant trend to workplaces requiring higher qualification. In 80% our interview partners were of opinion that the new jobs required a higher qualification, only in 20% they thought that the reverse would be true. We got no evidence for the so-called polarization thesis.

11. The trend to higher payment of the workers in connection with the implementation of information systems was stronger than the trend to lower payment. In about one quarter of our cases there was a rise of payments, whereas we had no case where payments were reduced.

12. Job enrichment by edp systems was estimated by about 60% of our interview partners. Only in 8 cases they guessed that the new jobs had poorer content.

13. Roughly 40% of our interview partners guessed that the new jobs cause more physical and psychical stress, approximately the same number of persons estimated that there was no change of stress.

14. Communication between employees remained without change in most cases. There was no evidence for the so-called isolation thesis, which we can often find in German assessment literature.

15. In 30% there is more performance control on the new jobs, but in most cases the additional measurements are not used to control the workers, but to review the capacity load of the system, e.g. the percentage of a terminal in a department. Moreover in some cases the measurements are used to control the performance of managers. In one case

we were told that labour representatives can use these edp reports to see whether the manager of the local warehouse of a chain has good figures because of this talent for good planning or because he exerts more pressure on his workers.

16. One of the most significant findings was that the older workers have more difficulties working with new information systems, especially display terminals. These difficulties lead to longer training times. But when the training is finished these older people seem to use the new instruments more intensively and more carefully than the younger employees.

17. When shop stewards participated in the implementation process, they had in almost all cases fruitful cooperation with managers. The question to the edp managers whether the monetary benefits of the new system, e.g. cost reduction, would have been higher if shop stewards would not have participated was answered in the negative in almost all cases.

18. In summary most workers are more content with the new computer-assisted jobs than with the old ones. But this was a question where the answers of the managers differed from those of the employees' representatives whereas in most other questions there were no great differences in the opinion pattern of edp managers and shop stewards.

19. In 60% of our cases there were complaints of single employees that they didn't get a display terminal for their workplace. You may find a lot of different explanations for this fact. But I think that a new instrument might not be so bad when so many people want it as early as possible.

Some of our results do not harmonize with opinions of many German critics of modern information technology. No wonder that I have a lot of reservations myself against contemporary assessment research or Wirkungsforschung. I shall publish them at another place.

G. Patrick Johnson*

Review of Selected Technology Assessment Studies of Information Technologies in the United States of America

*This paper was prepared with the assistance of Mark Abernathy of the Technology Assessment and Risk Analysis Group, NSF. The opinions, findings and conclusions are those of the author and do not necessarily represent those of National Science Foundation or any other agency of the U.S. Government.

Background

The National Science Foundation (NSF) has been actively involved in the support of technology assessments and associated research since 1971. Over one hundred projects have been supported through research awards totalling approximately ten million dollars. The program which directs this activity has evolved through several organizational identities, and is now in the Technology Assessment and Risk Analysis (TARA) Group. It is an element of the Division of Policy Research and Analysis (PRA) in the Directorate for Scientific, Technological, and International Affairs (STIA). Research which is supported by the TARA program is coordinated with other appropriate agencies, particularly the Office of Technology Assessment (OTA) of the Congress.

In addition to support of technology assessment on substantive topics such as new information technologies or other topics exemplified by TABLE 1, the TARA program also supports research on methodology and utilization for technology assessment and risk analysis.

This paper will review selected technology assessments in the information area for the purpose of drawing together some general themes which seem to be common, and are of interest from a public policy point of view.

Information as a TA Topic

During the decade since NSF began to make research awards to scientists for technology assessments, some eighteen projects have been supported which are associated with new information technologies. Information technologies have been specifically identified by the NSF technology assessment program in announcements for research proposals. In May, 1977 the program announcement identified four themes for assessment topics. One of these entitled <u>Automation, Cybernetics and Information Flow</u> was described as follows:

> Assessments in this thematic category would explore and analyze the impact of scientific advances in information systems and a variety of production and management systems. General topics might include: new technologies for production, processing, distribution, and utilization of information; new roles of information in society; artificial intelligence; regulatory alternatives for dealing with problems of information distribution and utilization; transdisciplinary, cross-modal, or multipurpose information systems; application of new technologies to production of goods and provision of services; new technologies for organizational management; marketing systems that will enhance delivery of goods and services among a variety of socioeconomic groups.(1)

In the current Program Announcement (December, 1978) the topic is described as follows:

> New Information Technologies. Research in the nature and structure of information promises to result in new technologies that will materially enhance our data processing capabilities. Such new capabilities can have a wide range of effects which may not be obvious to those involved in their development and implementation. Because the impacts of these technologies can significantly affect society's uses of information, it is important to undertake studies to foresee difficulties and seize new opportunities. Proposals should address information technologies that are likely to be deployed over the next decade. (2)

Information as a Resource.

In a recent article Anthony G. Oettinger, Chairman of the Program in Information Resources at Harvard University pointed out that "Every society is an information society and every organization an information organization." (3) He emphasizes the notion that information is a basic resource very much like natural resources such as energy and materials. But because of the fantastic engineering and scientific accomplishments in areas such as microelectronics, traditional ways of dealing with resource questions are not very relevant to information resources. In reviewing some of the technology assessments of information technologies there seem to be several common issues on which these anticipatory policy studies can focus. With proper attention, it is quite possible that our new information capabilities can be made to realize their great promise.

Problematic Issues for an Information Society.

As technology assessment has evolved in the United States, we have observed that at the root of most policy concerns about a technology is a problematic issue. The TARA program defines a problematic issue as a tradeoff question between desired goals, for example, productivity and safety or conservation and growth. (4) Several sets of problematic issues common to information technologies can be identified from the results of technology assessments which have been conducted in the United States. Most of the issues discussed below are included in each of the studies that are referenced. For discussion purposes, however, only one or two projects will be used for illustration.

Information Capability versus Information Access.

Very powerful new information capabilities resulting from the merger of computer and communications technologies are now becoming available. The new capabilities hold the promise for enabling users to be much better informed as citizens, consumers, and in educational, employment, and leisure activities. Two technology assessments illustrate some elements of the capability/access issue. An assessment of teletext and videotex technologies (5) now in progress examines, among other questions, issues with regard to alternatives for ownership and control of a variety of information services to the home and business. This assessment will shed light on relationships between ownership, marketing arrangements and capabilities which could be realized by the technologies. One of the policy questions emerging is the degree to which the potential of these new technologies can be achieved with and without regulatory controls. In the technology assessment of personal computers (6) the other side of the capability question was raised. That is, the differences among user capabilities and how these might lead to changes in social stratification based on the degree of information-richness or information-poverty of different sectors of society. Clearly, some important aspects of educational policy are involved on this point. The essence of this general issue is that a socially acceptable balance between realization of the full capability of information technologies and an open access to these capabilities for all will be a continuing matter for public policy concern.

Information Access versus Information Protection.

Many of the new information technologies provide the potential for very rapid and accurate communications of data and information. As access to these technologies expands, however, the potential for problems with regard to rights to privacy of information and data also arises. A study of the consequences of electronic funds transfer (7) points out that with this technology more detailed records will be in electronic form, so that they can be easily aggregated. More records of data will also pass through single nodes in electronic networks where they can be collected. Sources of data such as these open up possibilities that range from sale of specialized marketing-oriented mailing lists to blackmail. One of the most critical policy questions will be deciding what uses of data in such systems are legitimate and what uses should be prohibited. Because of threats to privacy it is quite likely that certain data and information in electronic funds systems will be given varying levels of protection. This observation is also valid for electronic mail (EM) systems. A technology assessment currently in progress is examining a number of policy aspects of electronic mail (8) and the provision of protection for EM systems equivalent to conventional mail systems is one of the important issues in that study.

Information Protection versus Institutional Functions.

Information is protected for two general reasons: because it contains value-sensitive information (e.g., purchase orders or funds tranfer orders) or because it contains privacy-sensitive information such as data on personal characteristics of people. One way to achieve protection for both types of information in electronic communication or computer systems is through a cryptographic approach. This approach can provide for both communication security (COMSEC) and protection for data stored in files (FILESEC). But in an assessment now in progress on the consequences of widespread uses of cryptography (9) by the public at large, new issues are emerging. The study is examining how the wide use of strong cryptography systems, such a public key codes, could change such things as the ability of law enforcement organizations to gather evidence through a search and discovery process. It is examining impacts, such as this, which could have an effect on a number of accepted and operational institutional procedures. For example, one feature of several of these systems is to provide digital signatures which authenticate, beyond any doubt, the sender and contents of a message. The study is also pointing out that one macro-effect of this technology could be to change a circumstance where a somewhat high probability of low value losses in conventional systems could become a lower probability occurrance, but of much higher loss value.

Production Efficiency versus Employment Stability.

New information technologies provide not only the potential for significantly enhanced communications and analysis capabilities, but also are being used in control of production processes. A technology assessment on the impact of robotics .(10) examined some issues with regard to change which could develop from application of robots, particularly in industrial batch processing. The study discusses the labor implications and concludes that before about 1995 there is not likely to be a severe labor force disruption from this technology. It suggests, however, that after that time there could be some important changes. Because robotic technology will not have the capability to deal with contingency situations, but must work under rather structured environmental circumstances, this could lead to a significant stratification in the production labor force. There could be large numbers of workers involved in menial tasks to structure the production environment for robots, with much smaller numbers of highly skilled workers performing supervision of the robots.

Another technology assessment addressed the general issue of the cross effects of telecommunications and transportation technologies. (11) Among other issues it pointed out how new telecommunications technologies could provide electronic access to jobs by handicapped persons and members of households who could perform "telework" from the home. The consequences of such applications will obviously be contingent on general economic and labor situations in the application areas. Shortages and excesses in labor force skills could be reinforced or smoothed depending on the general economic situation. In another set of assessments, (12, 13, 14) the special case of the scientific and technological information (STI) industry was addressed. These assessments analysed changes which could come about from new library strategies, by regulation of the STI industry as a public utility, and from new advances in areas such as micrography. Effects of such strategic changes as using S&T library systems as information warehouses or as information centers could have significant effects on the quality of research. Another assessment looked at the consequences which could arise from information system networks if used on a wide scale. (15) That project addressed problems such as those which arise when data are transferred across national boarders.

National Economic Interest versus International Cooperation.

One of the earliest NSF supported technology assessments covered the topic of remote sensing. (16) Because of the ability of satellite-based sensing technology to cover every part of the globe, this technology provides very significant capabilities for international cooperation in environmental monitoring programs and programs for resource management. However, it quickly becomes obvious that careful balancing between the interests of individual nations and global interests will be required.

Information Capabilities versus Institutional Functions.

The new capabilities for using information in new ways opens up the potential for change in a number of established institutions. Several technology assessments of information technologies have addressed such changes. Two assessments of communications advances postulate issues which could emerge from the video telephone (17) and from widespread uses of mobile communications. (18) Both of these could considerably reduce the need for face-to-face communication, and the effect on human communication could be significant, although subtle. These same technologies also raise issues with regard to liability when used, for example in medical diagnostics and treatment. An assessment of cable television (19) pointed out the potential for these systems to create changes in our educational institutions. An assessment of computer assisted makeup and imaging systems (CAMIS) (20) technology outlines a number of changes which could revolutionalize the printing and publishing industries. Long run effects of communication technology were explored in two retrospective technology assessments. (21, 22) In an historical study of the effects of undersea cable, for example, institutional changes were observed in international market systems, news services, diplomatic practices, naval strategy and in general and far reaching changes in the perceptions of time on a global scale.

The Need to Assess Information Technologies.

The great potential offered by the capabilities of new information technologies can be actualized into enormous benefits for society. But the consequences will undoubtedly involve significant institutional changes. The set of problematic issues discussed briefly above illustrates the range of public policy concerns that are imbedded in choices that move us toward an information society. Most of the changes in institutional arrangements implied by new information technologies could have major effects on how people will live their daily lives in the future. It seems then, that Symposia like this that lead to the kinds of research and analyses described above will be crucial inputs as choices about information technologies are debated and decided.

TABLE 1

EXAMPLES OF TOPICS OF NSF-SUPPORTED TECHNOLOGY ASSESSMENTS

Hail Suppression
Large Cargo Aircraft
Robotics
Quality of Work Life
Earthquake Prediction
Stratospheric Chlorofluoromethane
Structural Risks from Natural Hazards
Life Extending Technologies
Human Rehabilitation Techniques
Telecommunications-Transport Interactions
Science and Technology Informations Systems (STI): Services,
    Networking, Transfer, STI as a Regulated Public Utility,
    Technological Advances in STI, STI Library Systems
Snowpack Augmentation
Urban Solid Waste Management
No-Fault Insurance
Impact of Auto Regulation on Environment
Offshore Oil Operations
Advanced Automotive Propulsion
Video Telephone
Remote Sensing of Environment
Cable Television
Geothermal Development
Metric Conversion
Hydrogen Economy
Alternative Work Schedules
Electronic Funds Transfer
Biological Substitutes for Chemical Pesticides
Integrated Hog Farming

REFERENCES

(1) <u>Program Announcement, Technology Assessments in Selected Areas,</u> Division of Exploratory Research and Systems Analysis, National Science Foundation (NSF 77-25), Washington, D.C., May, 1977.

(2) <u>Program Announcement for Extramural Research</u>, Division of Policy Research and Analysis, National Science Foundation (NSF 78-78), Washington, D.C., December, 1978.

(3) Oettinger, A.G. "Information Resources: Knowledge and Power in the 21st Century", <u>Science</u>, Vol. 209, July 4, 1980.

(4) "Technology Assessment: A Brief Overview", Technology Assessment and Risk Analysis Group, National Science Foundation, March 1979.

(5) Tydeman, J. "Technology Assessment of Teletext and Videotex in the U.S.", NSF Research Award PRA 80-12731 (in progress) Institute for the Future, Menlo Park, California, Completion date February, 1982.

(6) Nilles, J. <u>A Technology Assessment of Personal Computers</u>, 3 volumes, University of Southern California, Los Angeles, September, 1980.

(7) Ernst, Martin L., <u>et al, The Consequences of Electronic Funds Transfer: A Technology Assessment of Movement Toward a Less Cash/Less Check Society</u>, Arthur D. Little, Inc., Cambridge, Massachusetts, June, 1975, U.S. Government Printing Office order number 038000-00429-0, NTIS No. PB 249128/OSL.

(8) Meyburg, A., _et al,_ "An Exploratory Analysis and Assessment of Electronic Message Transfer", NSF Research Award PRA 78-21171 (in progress), Cornell University, Ithaca, New York, Completion date July, 1981.

(9) Merkhofer, M.W., "Technology Assessments of Public Key Codes", NSF Research Award PRA 79-15143 (in progress) SRI International, Menlo Park, California, Completion date December 1981.

(10) Kurlat, S., Robert Gonsalves, and Harold Liff, _Technology Assessment: The Impact of Robotics,_ Eikonix Corporation, Burlington, Massachusetts, September, 1979, NTIS No. PB 80-142268.

(11) Harkness, R.C., _et al, Technology Assessment of Telecommunications - Transportion Interaction,_ 3 Volumes, SRI International, Menlo Park, California, May 1977, NTIS No. PB 272694/SL.

(12) Clayton, A. and Norman Nisenoff, _Potential Impacts of Automation and User Fees Upon Technical Libraries,_ Forecasting International Ltd., Arlington, Virginia, June, 1979, NTIS No. PB 271418/AS.

(13) Gellman, A.J. and Stephen Feinman, _Social Control of the Scientific and Technical Information System. Public Utility Regulation and International Transmissions - Final Report,_ Gellman Research Associates, Inc. Jenkintown, Pennsylvania, January, 1977, NTIS No. PB 279425.

(14) Stewart, D.E., _Technology Assessment of Advances in Scientific and Technical Information Services,_ Xerox Electro-Optical Systems, Pasadena, California, June, 1979, NTIS No. 241418/AS.

(15) Penniman, W.D., _et al_, Technology Assessment of Information Networking Technology, Battelle Columbus Laboratories, Columbus, Ohio, December 1976, NTIS No. PB 264188/AS.

(16) Zissis, G.J. Remote Sensing: A Partial Technology Assessment, Environmental Research Institute, University of Michigan, An Arbor, Michigan, May, 1977, NTIS No. PB 271278/4SL.

(17) Dickson, E.M. and R. Bowers, The Video Telephone: Impact of a New Era in Telecommunications, Praeger Publishers, New York, 1973.

(18) Bowers, R. et al, Communications for a Mobile Society: An Assessment of New Technology, Sage Publications, Beverly Hills, California, 1978.

(19) Ghandi, S.K. et al, Impact of Future Cable Television Technology, Rensselaer Polytechnic Institute, Troy, New York, 1976, NTIS No. PB 268465/2SL.

(20) Mayo, L. and Robert Anthony, An Exploratory Technology Assessment of Computer-Assisted Makeup and Imaging Systems, George Washington University, January, 1980.

(21) Coates, V.T. and B.S. Finn, A Retrospective Technology Assessment: Submarine Telegraphy, San Francisco Press, San Francisco, California, 1979.

(22) Pool, I. de S., Retrospective Technology Assessment of The Telephone, Massachusetts Institute of Technology, June, 1977, NTIS, No. PB. 280084/AS.

Ida R. Hoos

Pitfalls of Current Methodologies of Technology Assessment

Can We Avoid the Negative Effects of Information Technology?

Introduction

With a circularity bordering on incestuous validation, the
current methodology for the assessment of information technology virtually assures that there can be no escape from the
negative effects of an information society. This is so because both are manifestations of the same dominant paradigm.[1] They reflect the Zeitgeist which (a) gives impetus to
the ubiquitous development and application of information
technology and (b) provides the rationale whereby its effects
are assessed. And it is within that process of assessment
that information technology itself plays the central role.
Hence the circularity. It is due in large part to the techniques used that the effects known to be negative in the past
and even more portentous for the future are systemically and
systematically ignored. The "positive" side, readily ratio-
nalized in terms of cost/effectiveness, is gemütlich. A case
can always be made for higher productivity, speedier transmission, greater flexibility, and the like. But the other
side of the coin does not fit the analyst's model, for there
are no numbers to express the effects of information technology on every facet of our lives - as individuals, as workers, as citizens, and as members of society. Moreover, because the impacts will not be felt until some time in the future, the "facts" used in assessment come from fictional
scenarios that reflect the Weltanschauung of the assessor.
His model is a simulation of his own conception of reality.
Review of the salient characteristics of the assessment techniques and consideration of the areas of concern will provide us with a "social map" of the pitfalls.

---

1) T.S. Kuhn, The Structure of Scientific Revolutions, 3rd
   impression, University of Chicago Press, 1971, p. 175.

The Methodology

"Technology assessment is," according to Hetman,[1] "a systems analysis approach ... for decisions about the proper utilization of technology for social purposes." The connection between systems analysis and technology assessment renders the latter subject to the same shortcomings and vulnerable to the same criticisms as the former.[2] Forced into the structured model which typifies systems analysis (not as defined in broad philosophic terms but as practiced in the narrow "technical" sense), technology assessment cannot properly encompass factors which are intangible or immeasurable. At best, it can only encourage arbitrary assignment of values. Herein we see not only an inordinate opportunity for the analyst's own personal, subjective view to skew the assessment, but also a serious, albeit rarely acknowledged, deficiency in the methodology, which derives much of its prestige from its claims to "objectivity" and "rationality" when it is in essence a subjective exercise.

Nowhere is the potential for bias more insidious than in the crafting of the cost/benefit ratio, the mechanism by which trade-off is made between the presumably perceived advantages and disadvantages. The analyst exemplifies the poet's words,[3] he is, in the final analysis, the person he is -- technical in orientation, trained to accept the tools of his trade, and, subject to the cognitive economies each of us

---

1) Francois Hetman, Society and the Assessment of Technology, Organization for Economic Cooperation, Paris, 1973, p. 56.
2) Ida R. Hoos, Systems Analysis in Public Policy - A Critique, Berkeley, University of California Press, 1972.
3) "Du bist am Ende, was du bist".

learns to practice in his own profession,[1] prone to a certain amount of technical optimism. Understandably then, his cost/benefit calculations reflect his own conception, which he expresses in the only terms available to him -- dollars and cents. There then follows the "drunkard's search"[2] for data that "fit the model". (The frequency of benefit/cost ratios over one is not surprising in view of the common practice of having advocates or obedient consultants gather the data and perform assessments!) The "information system" forms a crucial element in the process of technology assessment and is, indeed, its main support mechanism. Hence, how it is conceived, designed, and operated and by whom have tremendous bearing on the conclusions emanating from the assessment. Generally, because information systems are designed by engineers, much attention is paid to the technical features -- storage capacity, ease of access, speed of transmission. Evaluation of the data as to validity, reliability, and accuracy is dismissed as irrelevant. There exists such a lack of trustworthiness of data that one authority,[3] pondering the question, who should "own" data, asked whether they were <u>worth</u> owning! Given the curiously involuted situation, we are, in fact, inviting foxes into the henhouse when we call

---

1) Amos Twersky and Daniel Kahneman, "Judgment Under Uncertainty: Heuristics and Biases,"Science, 27. September 1974, pp. 1124-31.
2) Abraham Kaplan tells the story of a drunkard searching, under a street lamp, for keys he had dropped some distance away. Asked why he didn't look where he had dropped them, he replied, "It's lighter here!"; The Conduct of Inquiry, Chandler Publishing Company., San Francisco, Calif., 1964, p. 11.
3) J. Ross Macdonald, (Chairman, Numerical Data Advisory Board, National Research Council) Editorial, "Are the Data Worth Owning?" Science, 30 June 1972, p. 1377.

upon systems analysts and other technical specialists to assess information technology.

Effects of Information Technology

No one knows, or has the means of measuring precisely, the effects of massive computerization on employment. Years ago, when electronic data processing first entered the commercial world, the gloomy prospect of job loss[1] was temporarily obscured and somewhat dispelled by the large army of machine-operators who replaced file clerks and book-keepers. All but ignored was the inexorable march toward more automation, with its evergreater potential for job displacement and, above all, for introducing enormous changes in job content and work environment. With every advance in information technology there has been further downgrading of skill, de-personalization, and dehumanization. For white-collar wor-kers, once the elite of the office force, the prime requi-sites are _Sitzfleisch_ and finger dexterity. Even if, as is confidently assumed by optimists, "telematics" will cause a dramatic increase in productivity, there is no reason to expect that there will occur somewhere in the labor market a compensating increase in new job opportunities. Quite the contrary. The simultaneous introduction of automation in the service sector and robotization in the industrial sector could so affect employment as to precipitate crises severe enough to jeopardize social stability. And these cannot be mitigated <u>unless the possibility of their occurring is ack-nowledged and offset by timely social planning</u>.[2] Besides the social upheaval caused by large-scale unemployment,

---

1) Ida R. Hoos, Automation in the Office, Washington, D.C., Public Affairs Press, 1961.
2) Simon Nora and Alain Minc, The Computerization of Society, Cambridge, Massachusetts, MIT Press, 1980, pp. 33 ff.

there are numberless deleterious assaults on the quality of life. Assessors of information technology would dismiss as externalities the statistics on alcoholism, drug abuse, and even crime as related to stressful working conditions. Nor can the value of personal privacy be factored into the cost/ benefit balance. But history tells us that even data collection that travels a benign course in the beginning can take on sinister and repressive tasks at a later time. Information technology in the form of data banks is a powerful instrument for social control. Political scientists warn that, quite contrary to the rosy prognostications of greater public involvement through electronic devices, politics in the post-industrial society will be strongly centralized and anti-democratic.[1]

Information technology so dominates public decision-making that every facet of our lives is affected. "Education technology" teaches our children the alphabet, hence they cannot read; "health technology" increases longevity but ignores the human care that the elderly need; "environmental impact statements" dictate irreversible courses of action without taking into account the long-term damage; "risk analyses", i.e. assessments of the impacts of <u>future</u> events,[2] guide us

---

1) Samuel P. Huntington, "Postindustrial Politics: How Benign Will It Be?", Comparative Politics, January, 1974, pp. 163-91.
2) Ida R. Hoos, "Reflections on and Implications of Systems Analysis as a Sociological Phenomenon", paper prepared for NATO Advanced Research Institute on Systems Analysis in Urban Policy-Making and Planning, Oxford, England, September, 1980; "Criteria for 'Good' Futures Research", Technological Forecasting and Social Change, Vol. 6, No. 4, August, 1974; "Some Fallacies in Futures Research", Technological Forecasting and Social Change, Vol. 10, No. 4, 1977.

to peace or war with a bravado born of ignorance.[1] Perhaps most to be deplored is the diminution of our critical faculties through the perpetual brainwash to which an electronic era subjects us. The "passivation"[2] that has occurred virtually precludes intelligent response. Not only are we incapable of making an unbiased assessment; we are discouraged from trying. The _vade_ _mecum_ environment interprets skepticism as a kind of subversion.

On the international scene global data flow has become an issue of paramount importance. Its dimensions dwarf trade wars of old and conjure up spectres of new spheres of influence, not all of them designed to maintain amical relations. Some of the concerns voiced include _de facto_ control by giant multi-national corporations, growing imbalance between have and have-not countries, potential for colonialism. New conceptions of dependence, independence, and interdependence are being formed with information as a base. The clamour for a "new world information order" only accentuates the disorder being caused by information technology. The abysmal inadequacy of methods to assess these consequences, taken in the context of the potential for terrorism, makes our society all the more vulnerable to the negative effects because ignorance renders us totally unprepared.

---

1) David Halberstam in The Best and The Brightest explicitly cites systems analysts as responsible for U.S. policy in Vietnam.
2) A term coined, I believe, by Jürgen Reese.

How to Get Good Research Results?

-Research Strategies and Special Issues-

Research strategies can be understood as sets of goal-oriented rules of behavior for research activities. The choice of the research strategy is a decisive factor for the success of the research project.

Efforts have been devoted within technology assessment to develop specific research methodologies. These methodologies usually consist of a series of steps considered to be necessary for carrying out investigations. But they can only be rough guidelines. The concrete research strategy has to be designed contingent on the nature of the technology, the perspectives of the research team, the degree of structure of the problem, the degree of detail already embedded in the problem definition, and so on.

Furthermore, while some aspects of a technology assessment project may be very ill-defined and unstructured other parts may be very specific and allow the application of formal methods. Any research strategy will therefore consist of various activities differing in their degree of specification regarding methods.

The first two papers of the third session deal with these problems of finding the right research strategy for impact research. Herbert Paschen, Bernd Wingert and Michael Rader give with their contribution "Some Remarks on Strategic Consideration for Technology Assessment" an overview of strategy problems within technology assessment and discuss especially the concept of "Begleitforschung". Norbert Szyperski and Ursula M. Richter emphasize in "A Constructive Approach for Impact Research on Information Technology" the need for a policy directed strategy for impact research and present some aspects which have to be considered within such an approach.

Issues of research strategies related to the validity and acceptance of the results are the topic of the remaining four articles.

Horstfried Läpple asks in "Anticipating Future Use of Technology - Factors Influencing Technology Transfer in General and from Government R&D Agenices in Particular" for possibilities of improving the knowledge about technology transfer mechanism in order to improve the quality of anticipating new fields of technology applications.

In many instances democratic values demand public participation in impact research. And indeed the public has often the knowledge and the moral right to participate. But there are tremendous practical problems if the representatives of the public are to avoid being placed in a hostage situation. Niels Bjørn-Andersen examines in his contribution "Public Participation in Technology Assessment" the necessary prerequisites for coping with these difficulties.

Research on technological impacts pursues often very pragmatic objectives. Because of scarce financial resources for research it is a major issue to find the most urgent or most important problems and to develop priority lists for research. Riccardo Petrella presents in his essay "The Practice of Project Choice and Assessment - The FAST Programme" the identification and design of the EEC research programme.

The final paper by Francois Hetman "Some Glimpses on the International Co-operation in R&D" takes up the problems and conditions for succesful multinational research. International co-operation is necessary for many projects on information technology because its impacts and causes are by no means restricted by national boundaries. Efficient problem-solving in such instances needs to be intergovernmental.

In the discussion three topics have been of main interest:
- The influence of the different parties involved on the
  research results
- The possibility of having public participation in
  research
- The possibilities and objectives for carrying out
  international technology assessment activities.

(1) Neutrality of Research

Within the impact research community there exist contrary
opinions about the aspect of neutrality of research. Several
problem layers have to be distinguished here.

o Shall the researcher be neutral?
  Technology assessment results are used not only to get a
  more complete picture of the decision problem, but are
  often used directly in the political process to support
  one or more issues. Therefore, there is a danger that
  results may be presented out of their context in order to
  support certain preconceived opinions. This political role
  of technology assessment should never be ignored. Some
  researchers consider it mandatory that the values and
  objectives are specifically stated from the beginning.
  Others think, that in many cases it is necessary for the
  researcher to act as spokesperson for a certain group,
  e.g., if one is working on assessing the impacts of a particular technology on a particular (underprivileged)
  group. In this way one gives up the assumption of "objective" research. This position means a clear shift from a
  traditional positivistic scientitic point of view towards
  an action-oriented strategy often based explicitly on
  increased involvement of researchers in political processes.

In the more "traditional" view, the prime objective of the researcher carrying out technology assessment is to be as neutral as possible. This is the case of assessments sponsored by the Office of Technology Assessment of the USA. This means that all underlying assumption have to be made apparent and that all aspects, whether they are valued as negative or positive by the one party or the other, have to be investigated and presented in a neutral and objective form.

o Can the researcher be neutral?
  Objectivity in the results is not only a question of the desirability but also of capability. A first restriction can be seen in the education and training of the researcher which means that an engineer and a sociologist will probably see the particular problem with two different perspectives. As pointed out earlier there are some possibilities of reducing this kind of influence, e.g. to carry out interdisciplinary teamwork.

Secondly the sponsor of the research project has a major influence on the kind of results coming out of the investigation. This potential influence can be exerted in several ways:
  . the choice of the research team might already define the basic direction of the results through defining the perspective,
  . the sponsor can make expectations explicit to the research team, and the research team might work accordingly ("whose bread I eat, his song I sing"),
  . the problem definition of the research task may be defined so narrowly as to exclude major critical issues.
This last point especially seems to be a problem because it is so difficult to recognize. Even if the problem definition is broadend, the designer of a research programme is burdened with an enormous amount of responsibility for taking "all aspects into account".

o Are the results used in a neutral way?
  Most of the current technology assessments are done on
  subjects where "battlelines" are already drawn. It seems
  that there is no chance for neutrality where conflicting
  goals are recognized.

(2) Public Participation

Participation is necessary in technology assessment for a
lot of reasons, and its necessity is not questionned within
the impact research community. But the problem is how and to
what extent the public should participate. It is not
possible and certainly not efficient to let the whole public
participate in technology assessment. It has to be decided
from study to study who should participate in which way, and
at which time. Especially it is important to discuss how to
provide the public with a vehicle for taking part without
becoming hostages, i.e. without becoming victims of beeing
convinced to accept a development which might be contrary to
their "objective interest.

The question "who decides" is here again an important one.
Guidelines and rules for involving the public in the decision process do not exist. Different models of participation
have been practised with varying success but general recommendations are yet to be derived.

Participation can be very helpful in overcoming certain
limitations on the part of the experts. Experts are often
completely unqualified to foresee how people will use or
misuse technologies. Important impacts are therefore missed.
Non-experts who are not conditioned to expect particular
impacts may therefore be more qualified to identifying the
unexpected.

On the other hand participation requires often a high degree of knowledge about the technology in question and the involvement of non-experts turns out to be inefficient in these cases, unless the public gets its own "counter experts".

The problem of public participation in technology assessment often boils down to political discussions. One must be aware for political reasons and that these positions are not questionned.

(3) International Technology Assessment

International research in the sense that the EEC sees its task, does not mean the attainment of a certain set of objectives. Rather it is to identify critical issues for the Community. Technology assessment in this context is not used as a political tool, except perhaps to further European integration. The problems of setting the priorities for research projects and of evaluating results are extremely difficult. The urgency of certain problems and their consequences differ from country to country within the Community.

There have been few research projects with two or more nations participating. Needs and possibilities for multinational technology assessments should therefore be examined more carefully. The current restrictions for international research in the sense of financial constraints are mostly caused by the organizational constraints of the governments which are not set up to pay their main attention to strategic questions. It ought to be possible to overcome that restriction within the EEC.

H. Paschen, B. Wingert, M. Rader

Some Remarks on Strategic Considerations for Technology Assessment

1. Introduction

(1) TA practitioners are often in the kind of situation psychologists would describe as an aversion-aversion conflict: If they try to apply the standards dictated by the fairly sophisticated expectations that were raised with regard to TA before the setting up of OTA they are almost doomed to failure when applying these standards in actual projects. On the other hand, when they choose to ignore the majority of the theoretical and methodical demands and attempt to tackle a given problem with the available knowledge they are certain of severe criticism after the event. In the first case, they are losing the game against reality, in the second case, they are losing the game for their reputation. Recent criticism has increasingly sought to defeat concrete TA-projects on a third ground, namely that of classifying the game as lost from the outset, at best calling it rhetoric (cf. Wynne 1975).

(2) It is best not to be too pessimistic about this. If we consider it useful to conduct technology assessments despite such criticism, it is important to develop strategies which are neither characterized by too great dependence on theory nor by sheer pragmatism. From the beginning of the debate on TA, practical interest was focused on the techno-economic and social development of industrialized countries; TA was regarded as a means for the improved control of this development. The idea was to consider the consequences of technical and socio-economic innovation <u>to a greater extent</u> than previously and <u>before their realization</u> by means of feeding knowledge into existing decision-making structures. The institutionalization of the Office of Technology Assessment in the U.S.A. is one possible solution. Regardless of whether one considers the work of this office as suc-

cessful or not, it is important to realize that the character of politics is undergoing change by means of this new institution. Since the investigation of unintended side effects and delayed effects are expressly made an issue, governmental and parliamentary decision-makers are assuming the role of an instance to which the responsibility for such consequences may legitimately be attributed. This process of attributing the responsibility for consequences can not, however, be carried on endlessly, i.e. to the nth-order effects (cf. Tribe 1973, Bechmann/Wingert 1980). In addition, TA is carried out _within_ a given society. It is therefore no less influenced by society's structures and conflicts of interest than other subsystems. Critical evaluations of TA should always consider this condition, however tempting the idea of a helmsman outside of society may be.

2. <u>The concept of strategy and the point of reference for</u>
    <u>this paper</u>

(3) The aim of this contribution is certainly not to propose a <u>single</u> strategy for technology assessment or to sketch the outlines of a Guidebook for TA-studies (cf. Porter, Rossini, Carpenter and Roper 1980). Experience gathered up to now would suggest that there is no <u>one</u> strategy for TA-studies and that a suitable strategy must be developed for each of them. It is only possible to set up guidelines for the development of appropriate strategies. The development of adequate differentiations and, even more so, retaining such guidelines as regulative ideas during an actual TA project are complex learning processes which even TA practitioners may command only after much practice.

(4) The first question to be discussed is: What is meant by

"strategy"? And which basic strategic considerations have to be made in connection with a TA?

In management science, the term "strategic" or "long-range planning" is used to denote the planning dealing "with decisions regarding the broad technological and competitive aspects of the organization, the allocation of resources (human and material) over an extended period, and the long-run integration of the organization within its environment" (Kast/Rosenzweig 1970, p. 444 f.). Other forms of planning, such as tactical and operational planning, are conducted <u>within the frame-work</u> of the strategic plan.[1]

Others, like Niklas Luhmann define planning as "deciding on decisions" (1966, p. 67). An important element in this concept of planning is that "on the one hand definitive decisions are made, on the other hand, however, that these do not make later decisions redundant or completely determine their contents, leaving them open so that later decisions are necessary" (op. cit., p. 67). Planning is not, however, every form of determining preconditions for decisions. One may speak of planning only if and when one is dealing with the definition of a problem and with the conditions for its solution (cf. op. cit., p. 68).

(5) This conception of strategy as a framework plan on the one hand and as "deciding on decisions" on the other hand may be further clarified if we consider work on the theory of human action (cf. Miller, Galanter and Pribham 1960, 1973; Volpert 1980). Here we conceive strategy as

---

1) A similar conception of strategic planning is described by Kirsch and others (1979).

a meta plan. Plans are designs and programmes for action. They guide the actions of individual or collective systems. The term "framework plan" is usually employed to designate the part of a plan describing long-range aims or higher-order conditions. Meta plans are plans for the development of more sophisticated plans. These terms may be meaningfully employed to describe the actions of individuals as in psychology (cf. op. cit.) and to describe the actions of complex social systems (cf. Luhmann 1966).[1]

Examining TA from this point of view thus implies considering those conditions and factors which may prevent the TA from achieving its goals and accomplishing its tasks. Such conditions may be related to the sponsor and users of TA, to the problem or the task in hand, to the methods and to the role the TA-team assumes. These are the aspects that will be discussed at greater length in

---

1) Miller, Galanter and Pribham (1973) discuss meta plans in connection with the problem of organizing learning matter during the phases of acquisition and memorizing in such a manner that it may be embedded into higher order structures, thus aiding the process of learning (cf. p. 125f.). The ability to construct meta plans may be attributed to the possibility of realising a hierarchical organization of activities. In this context they use "strategy" to denote the molar units encompassing smaller "molecular" tactical and operative units (cf. p. 26): A meta plan is not simply a phase in this hierarchy (in this case one should better employ the term framework plan), but a plan for a plan (cf. p. 172f.). Thus, a mathematical proof may be regarded as a plan to organize mathematical terms and symbols that are themselves plans. Eventually the hierarchy of plans results in heuristics, since the method of finding a heuristic plan is itself heuristics (cf. p. 174).

the following.

(6) Strategic considerations related to TA may be divided
    into 3 main groups:

Class 1 There have been many controversies on TA and a great
        number of studies within the last 10 years or so.
        This history of TA could be examined with the aim of
        finding out whether factual performance can be mea-
        sured against the original goals and whether the
        self-perception inside the TA-community is under-
        going a change. One may interpret the contribution
        by Nehnevajsa and Menkes (1980) in this sense when
        they distinguish different types of TA.[1]

Class 2 TA itself may be seen as a strategic conception of
        increasing the conciousness for consequences of poli-
        tical action. It may be regarded in relationship to
        other conceptions (e.g. "Begleitforschung", BF[2]),
        which are aimed more at illuminating the depth struc-
        ture of human action when utilizing technology.

---

1) I: going beyond considerations of economic feasibility;
   II: with heavy emphasis on the comprehensive identification and analysis of the full range of social, economic,
   and environmental effects of technological inducements;
   III: with emphasis on contingency analysis, attempting
   to bound the study deliberately and not through default;
   IV: stressing organizational, institutional and persona-
   lity-related aspects of decisionmaking.
2) In the following, we have employed the German term "Begleitforschung" (BF) to denote assessments "accompanying"
   the implementation process. A suitable English term does
   not exist: impact analysis is too broad a translation and
   implementation analysis too narrow.

<u>Class 3</u> Strategic considerations and decisions must also be carried out <u>within</u> TA studies.

In the following, we shall be confining ourselves to classes 2 and 3.

We propose to regard TA and BF as two methods of illuminating human action. TA does this by considering human action by its effects and by analysing alternatives for action, BF does so by analyzing the <u>process</u> of developing and realizing action programmes in a given situation. The following discussion will be concerned more with TA.

3. <u>TA and BF as strategic conceptions of analysis</u>

(7) Generally, technology assessments have two main subjects: the effects of a technology or of the application of a technology and the decision-making system (policy analysis) for the particular area of technology. While it is easy to name the respective subjects, in many cases it is difficult to find solid boundaries for the technological area as well as for the decision-making system. Concentrating for the moment on the latter, it is evident that the decision-making system does not merely consist of those people who are in the formal position to legitimately decide technological matters. Both public and private interest groups should be involved in the TA-decision-making system, if not in the formal sense, then on a consultative basis. This is because they may actively attempt to influence the decision process on account of their power or backing in the population and thus create relevant conditions for decision-making. Yet another component has to be added: those people affected by the use of a technology in some way or other, but not sufficiently well organized to enact an effi-

cient role in the technology design power play.

One first remark is concerned with TA as the producer of options and as a cross-sectional balancing method: TA does not have the task of replacing legislative, administrative or political decisions but of improving the level of information and of making the premises for decision transparent. Obviously, the conscientious compilation of available knowledge on a technology at a given time can serve to prejudice the relevant decision-makers. The result of a policy-analysis of a TA is, however, not the one best way but a series of options for action. Similarly, it is not usually the task of a TA to produce novel information on effects, but to organize existing knowledge and to expose gaps in existing knowledge and research. Thus, an important result of a TA may be the initiation of research programmes. The task of a TA may be described roughly as follows: It should record the available knowledge on the effects of technologies (including gaps in this knowledge) in a manner relevant to decision-making in a kind of balance-sheet. TA may be characterized as a cross-sectional, balancing method of research related to decision-making.

(8) The second remark concerns BF as a complement to TA, as a "longitudinal" analysis. As already explained, the term "Begleitforschung" is used in German-speaking countries to denote studies on technological projects, accompanying the process of technology use and implementation by scientific analyses.

Reference to a process of technology use and design may be regarded as characteristic. Within this framework, even minor developments of technology may be dealt with.

However, the main task of "Begleitforschung" is to assist the development of an economically feasible compromise between technical potential, organizational requirements and the needs of those affected. Thus, the main task is not, as in a TA, to carry out a comprehensive analysis of effects as an aid for decision-making but to design a complex system. Whereas TA is normally conducted under pressure to decide with time limitations, "Begleitforschung" also presents the opportunity to deal with research problems. On the other hand, "Begleitforschung" is in greater danger than TA of being worn out in the process of negotiation on the design of technology. In the Federal Republic of Germany, "Begleitforschung" is conducted to a large extent in the confines of the Federal government's "humanization of working life" programme.

(9) The third remark concerns the idea of "repeated" TAs, which is a good idea and may be traced to recommendations by the National Academy of Engineering (1969). However, the interplay between (cross-sectional, balancing) TAs and (longitudinal, analytical) "Begleitforschung" would appear more suited to assess the complex effects of modern technology, in particular of data processing (Paschen, Bechmann, Wingert, 1980, deal with this subject at greater length).

(10)Whilst Porter, Rossini, Carpenter and Roper (1980) see close connections between TA and "environmental impact analysis", they do not succumb to the temptation of mixing both conceptions. Special attention should be paid to varying accents in other conceptions. This applies especially to "innovation research", which analyses conditions favorable or unfavorable to the adoption of innovations and their diffusion. The main focus of attention is the success of techno-organizational changes, whether these are accompanied by negative or delayed unintentional effects or not. "Evaluation research" is concerned with measuring the actual effects of programmes as compared with their goals and with attempting to relate these to causes. Similarly, "implementation research" is concerned with the actual effects of programmes, however, seeking to trace them back through the jungle of responsibilities and regulations, thus, as TA, making an issue of political and administrative decision-making (cf. Mayntz 1977). "Impact research" (cf. Reese et al. 1978) is being discussed in the field of information technology and is attempting to combine a number of strands, without yet leading to a coherent conception. Finally, "action research" is developing very radical standards for alternative research practice and methods (Haag et al. 1975, Moser and Ornauer 1978).

Reference to these differing varieties has not been prompted by the desire to preserve chances of academic differentiation. Each of the approaches has its own tradition, the knowledge of which may sharpen our senses for methods of dealing with problems.

4. <u>Strategic decision points in TA and BF</u>

4.1 <u>Research strategic decisions related to the potential users and sponsors of TA.</u>

(11)Technology assessment involves what have been described as two communities: On the one hand the assessors as producers of the study, on the other, the potential users of the study. The analysis of the situation of decision-makers from a strategic point of view means conceiving their decision-making behavior as a variable dependent on conditions of the decision problem, on the given situation and on the personalities of the persons involved. This perspective and functional modelling give the TA team space to maneuver because they allow prognostic conclusions concerning the future behavior of the decision-makers. On the other hand, the complementary effect for the TA team is that the assumption of a role may no longer be determined adequately by the trustful exposure of all considerations made in the TA analysis procedure. The TA team must rather view its own input as an independent variable and behave accordingly. At best, the blind sense of companionship with the decision-makers is to be described as naive since it fails to take into consideration the widely varying conditions for action of the decision-maker and the analysis team. The situation is further complicated by the fact that TAs are typically addressed to several users. Porter et al. have made a list of potential users of a TA/EIA, some of whom are decision-makers whilst others are not:

- The sponsoring organization
- Other executive agencies
- Other executive branch units
- Legislative bodies
- Private interests
- Public interests
- The research community.
    (cf. Porter et al. 1980, p. 405).

Obviously, the reconstruction of the decision-making situation for individual actors and the construction of a model for their interplay is by no means a trivial task.

(12) The utilization of any given TA-study depends to a great
extent on establishing an effective flow of communications between the two communities of TA producer and
TA users. Theories on barriers to communication can be
classified in 3 categories, suggested by Caplan et al.
(1975):

(1) Knowledge-specific theories: major barriers to utilization are created by research producers. Such
barriers include disciplinary narrowness, ideological bias, too strong emphasis on quantifiability,
lack of policy orientation, methods, data etc.

(2) Policy-maker constraint theories: demand for over-
simplified information, time limitations, organizational and political factors.

(3) Two-communities theories: this perspective emphasizes mismatches between producers and potential users
in such areas as language, values, goal, methods to
be employed, standards of quality and significance.

Assessments may either be used to influence thinking
(conceptual consequences) or to have identifiable impact on policy decisions (instrumental consequences).
In practice, however, TA is used mainly as a source for
background information and rarely as a basis for decision-making. Greater effect was achieved with TA studies
by bringing issues to the attention of the decision-
makers than it was by selecting options. However, it is
to be expected that improved assessments will contribute
more to decision-making.

For the moment, we shall concentrate on the issue of "effective communication", which is very difficult to bring about in practice.

(13)A review of 15 studies conducted by the OECD (1978) came to the conclusion that:

"It is practically impossible to trace any attempt to establish a permanent interplay between the analysts and the decision-makers. The former seem to proceed with their investigations almost exclusively on their own grounds, avoiding the area of decision-making" (OECD, p. 84).

(14)We shall now focus our attention on the problem of establishing an effective flow of communications between the TA team and the various parties having interest in the subject under review. These parties would have justification for their rejection of a TA team's findings if they felt that facts and arguments were inadequately collected in the first place.

To start off with, we shall look into the advantages and disadvantages of charging TA teams with varying degrees of dependence on the sponsor with conducting a TA. These are summed up at greater length in Paschen et al. (1978, pp. 50 et seq.). The key issues are, among others:

- The credibility of results for the sponsor and interested parties;

- real or perceived pressure to bias results on behalf of the sponsor or interested parties;

- the power of the sponsor to suppress results perceived
  as unfavorable;

- the coordination and management of the assessment,
  particularly if sponsor and TA team have no close
  ties;

- the adaptability in regard to resources and deadlines
  if these vary considerably from the estimates before
  the outset of the assessment.

TA studies may be conducted "in house", i.e. by teams
belonging to the institution sponsoring the assessment,
or by independent contractors, most often commercial
research institutes.

Whereas TAs conducted by teams from inside sponsoring
institutions do have the advantage of close links with
the sponsor and thus of the potential for constant feedback to satisfy the sponsor's intentions, this could
also lead to distrust on the part of interested parties
who perceive their own interests as being at odds with
the sponsor's intentions. Possible consequences of this
distrust are refusal to cooperate by providing
information and opinions and ignoring the results and
recommendations of the assessment on the grounds that
just these opinions and facts have not been taken into
consideration. There is some justification for such
mistrust, since "in house" teams could feel some obliga-
tion to bias their results in favor of the perceived
interests of the sponsoring agency. Another argument
levelled against "in-house" teams is that these seldom
cover all the scientific disciplines involved and that
they are often lacking in experience and expertise to
conduct high-quality assessment. Insufficient scientific

quality is, of course, another reason for groups seeing assessment results as unfavorable to reject these results.

Whilst these disadvantages seem to speak in favor of contracting TAs to institutes outside of the sponsoring agency, one obvious drawback of this procedure is the insufficient communication between sponsor and contractor which could, once again, lead to an assessment's results being ignored. Admitting representatives of the sponsoring agency to the research team could solve some of the problem, but the "participation" of other groups in the form of information inputs may nevertheless quite easily lead to the assessment developing into directions not envisaged at all by the sponsor when planning the assessment.

What of truly neutral institutes? This may be a rhetoric question as there would appear to be very few, if any, truly independent and neutral institutes, since they are all dependent on contracts from government and industry. This also means that they are subject to severe financial restraints and limits on the time they may spend for a given assessment and they are thus forced to compromise with regard to the quality of the assessment. The demand for neutrality and independence could, in the present circumstances, most readily be satisfied by groups from universities. However, government agencies often hesitate to give contracts to universities on grounds of lack of management expertise and capacity. In addition, the organization of universities, at least in the Federal Republic of Germany, impedes rather than encourages the formation of multi-discipline teams.

The OTA represents an attempt at linking institutionalized technology assessment and political decision-ma-

king. One desired effect of OTA's work is to raise the
level of sophistication of political debate, thus contributing to the improved functioning of a democratic
society. Experience with the OTA has shown that even an
agency of this kind can fall into the trap of working
too close to the day-to-day action of Congress, or, on
the other hand, of drifting "too far away from the legislative pattern of doing things" (Government Executive,
Sept. 1980). With regard to parliamentary systems such
as that in the Federal Republic of Germany, a senior
member of OTA staff has suggested that since the governing party has special access to the resources of the
ministries, an OTA-type of organization should choose
issues for study that lie quite far in the future. The
studies should deal with topics whose impacts will occur
between five and ten years after the study is completed
(personal communication).

(15) Potential users of a study can have much the same biasing effect as a sponsor, sometimes assuming the role of
a quasi-sponsor if allowed to do so by the producer and
the main sponsor. Another effect is that the information
collecting process can be biased by the results expected
by the interest group involved. An obvious example is
information being supressed if perceived as being unfa-
vourable to the group's interest. Phenomena of this kind
are by no means confined to private or public interest
organizations. Examples have been reported of government
agencies impeding or influencing information collection
for studies conducted on behalf of other government
agencies. This especially applies to countries with
federal governmental systems, where a state is often
governed by different parties than those in power in
central government.

(16) In order to be truly useful for policy makers, TAs should

provide a concise overview of all relevant facts and opinions on the subject of the assessment. They should also be acceptable to the interest groups involved, i.e. the groups should feel that they have a fair chance of their points of view being given due consideration. One of the most important prerequisites for the fulfilment of these conditions is that the TA team have free access to the necessary information. This may be achieved only if the institution conducting the TA has both the degree of independence from the sponsor or interested parties and the reputation for scientific quality to ensure objective and neutral fact-gathering. Ideally, the reports by such an institution should provide the decision-makers and the public wishing to participate in the decision making process with adequate, balanced information on the pros and cons of alternative policy opinions. It would also be ideal if the institution had the necessary funds to decide on the size of the assessment.

In democratic systems, it is a tempting idea to set up a neutral institution for conducting TAs with responsibility to parliament. In the view of limited resources, a body must be set up to make decisions on the subjects for assessment and on the allocation of available resources. A board of governors could be composed by members of the political parties represented in parliament, assuming that these represent the entire spectrum of opinion on any issue involved and that they will ensure that all relevant information is made available. However, experience with similarly composed governing bodies has been far from encouraging, at least in the Federal Republic of Germany, e.g. for public radio and TV companies. They have merely been used as a further field for conflict between opposing parties, so that part of the discussion, i.e. that of members of the same party with widely differing opinions, is removed from the boards to party meetings. The composition of boards with representatives of interest groups poses the problem of deciding on which groups should participate and on size (managability). Also, experience has shown that this kind of board is most generally composed by party affiliation.

In practice there are bound to be many drawbacks and setbacks before TA plays the part we would wish for. Additionally, it is to be feared that in times of decreased public spending on social services, technology assessments, and especially the setting up of new institutions to carry them on, are going to be very low on the politicians' priority lists.

4.2 Research strategic considerations in relation to the problem

(17) In the literature, it has been said that "The first step in contemplating assessment ... is to challenge its existence" (Porter et al. 1980, p. 65). Furthermore, it is pointed out that exact bounding is necessary in regard to time horizon, the spatial extent of the impacts, the institutional involvements, the range of applications considered in TA, the impact sectors and the policy options. This advice to challenge the problem definition is important and is in accordance with experience to be gathered in systems analysis. It is the task of the TA team to elaborate its own and independent definition of the problem and to gather information on it in order to interpret any given articulation of the problem.

One of the most important questions in a TA is to what extent it should be burdened with unsolved research questions. Another important point is related to the degree of consensus or of disagreement concerning the status of the problem. It should be pointed out that the very definition of an issue as a "problem" can lead to controversy if interest groups are affected. TA occasionally is confronted with the accusation that it itself contributes to "waking sleeping dogs", thus creating a situation which might otherwise never have come about. There is no simple strategy to escape from this kind of situation. The assembly of a circle of experts to discuss such open questions may even contribute less to better understanding of the problems involved than to a better documentation of points of disagreement.

(18) A further strategic question in the assessment of problems is related to whether a TA should produce an independent, concrete scenario (e.g. on energy supply). If one does this, one generally has to prove the validity of such a scenario and to achieve consensus on one's own assessment of the problem. Another possibility is to proceed from the scenarios being discussed in any actual given situation and to use them as a point of departure for analysis. A third possibility is to resort to a normative scenario, i.e. not to examine where current developments could lead to, but to ask where we want to go to in the face of a given situation. Obviously, the question of the basis for social consensus is equally controversial in this context. It would be pointless to base an analysis on goals that very few would wish to achieve.

(19) Of further significance for the strategic assessment of problems is the distinction introduced by the Study by the National Academy of Engineering between technology-initiated TA, problem-initiated TA and project-initiated TA. We are thus concerned with describing the type of problem: are we concerned with the technology itself and

its adequate development and utilization (e.g. currently cable television, where the range of possible applications is very broad indeed); or are we concerned with certain problems and effects created by the utilization of technology so that, in extreme cases, alternative solutions must be developed; or, finally, are we concerned with the assessment of effects caused in a concrete, spatially restricted project related to a specific technical application, where we have to work our way through many areas of impact, but where the impact domain is clearly bounded?

The identification of critical points, as described in (17) - (19), may be achieved fairly simply. However, it is far more difficult to design a strategy for finding a way out of a given problem situation. In this case, the TA team is forced to lean on general principles of heuristics and to otherwise rely on its own imagination. Unfortunately, a general methodology of dealing with problems has yet to be developed.

4.3 Research strategic considerations in relation to the methods

(20) The strategic character of the TA conception is most visible in the way individual methods and techniques are applied. This is the area where the greatest demands are made on the competency of the TA team since it must have command over a large variety of methods and be able to apply them adapted to the problems.

Recently, the question of methods has been discussed particularly in connection with suggestions for the evaluation of the TA-studies themselves. The debate on advantages and disadvantages of experimental studies, previously conducted for evalutation research, is here being revived (cf. Weiss 1974). The main difficulty lies in the development of higher-order points of reference and thus not merely in the problem of the internal and external validity but in that of, for example, the utility of TA-studies (cf. Porter and Rossini 1977, Koppel 1979; Connolly, Porter and Rossini 1979; Porter, Rossini, Carpenter and Roper 1980, chap. 18).

(21) An excellent discussion of the problem of adapting methods applied to a given situation is conducted for evaluation research by Wollmann and Hellstern (1977). It is of little use to argue the superiority of experimental designs if the given situation is unsuited to implementing such a design. In this kind of situation one may often only resort to less sophisticated case study approaches. The application of formal decision models must also be determined by the given problem, and not viceversa. What can be gained from the application of these methods is not a definite answer to a question but rather the explication of the decision-making premises of the decision-makers (cf. especially Ida Hoos 1979). The decisive step remains that of judgement: "Above all and most important, judgement is the crucial ingredient" (op. cit., p. 192).

4.4 Research strategic considerations in relation to the role of the TA and BF team

(22) The question of an adequate role for a TA team depends to a large extent on the team's capability to develop for itself an adequate model of the decision-making situation (cf. Bozeman and Rossini 1979), and to reduce rivalry with the decision-makers, but simultaneously to collect information on important premises for decision-

making. This role problem is even more crucial for a BF team; it is of vital importance for its "survival" in the process of negotation on the design of technology. In the confines of a TA, the participation of diverging opinions may be employed as a strategy to balance these opinions against each other. The TA team may accept or even promote the participation of diverging opinions in, for example, a consultative board as a strategy to balance these interests against each other. There is a good chance for TA to win this game, at least temporarily. On the other hand, the same strategy may lead to undesirable results for the BF team because it is far more complicated to stick to a well-defined role over a two or three years' process of negotiating the technological design.

Schacht (1977), drawing on his own experience in a complex BF-project on the introduction of data-processing technologies in the health service, has identified two equally dangerous roles for BF. The first of these is to force the BF team into the role of a service group for collecting data and working one's way through alternatives, but excluding the BF team from the actual negotiation processes. The second of them is to force "Begleitforschung" into the role of the auditor whose task is to measure results against the declared goals, so that important channels to data and information rapidly dry up.

(23) Defining a concrete role for TA or BF is in itself a methodological problem. One cannot sufficiently grasp the interplay between politics and research by means of an appeal: "This interaction takes place on both social and intellectual planes and should include efforts by both groups to understand each other's underlying values" (Bozeman and Rossini 1979, p. 34). The theoretical question remains how the legitimacy of the given method of problem solution may be justified.

References

BECHMANN, G. und WINGERT, B.:
Technology Assessment als Rationalisierung technologiepoli-
tischer Entscheidungsprozesse, in: J. Mathes (Hrsg.), Ver-
handlungen des 20. Deutschen Soziologentages. Frankfurt
a.M.: Campus 1981, 314-328

BOZEMAN, B. and ROSSINI, F.A.:
Technology Assessment and Political Decision-Making. Technological Forecasting and Social Change 15 (1979), 25-35

CAPLAN, N., et al.:
The Use of Social Science Knowledge in Policy Decisions at
the National Level.
Ann Arbor: Center for Research on Utilization of Scientific
Knowledge, Institute for Social Research, University of
Michigan, 1975

CONNOLLY, T., PORTER, A.L., ROSSINI, F.A.:
On the Evaluation of Assessment and Assessments.
Technological Forecasting and Social Change 15 (1979), 73-76

Facing Up to the Realities of Finiteness.
The Government Executive Sep. 1980 (reprint)

HAAG, F., KRÜGER, H., SCHWÄRZEL, W., WILDT, J. (Hrsg.):
Aktionsforschung, Forschungsstrategien, Forschungsfelder und
Forschungspläne.
München: Juwenta 1975 (2. Aufl.)

HOOS, I.:
Societal Aspects of Technology Assessment.
Technological Forecasting and Social Change 13 (1979), 191-202

KAST, F.E. and ROSENZWEIG, J.E.:
Organization and Management.
New York: McGraw-Hill 1970

KIRSCH, W., ESSER, W.-M., GABELE, E.:
Das Management des geplanten Wandels von Organisationen.
Stuttgart: Poeschel 1979

KOPPEL, B.:
Evaluating Assessment: A Comment and a Perspective.
Technological Forecasting and Social Change 14 (1979),
147-152

LUHMANN, N.:
Politische Planung (1966), in: N. Luhmann: Politische Pla-
nung - Aufsätze zur Soziologie von Politik und Verwaltung.
Opladen: Westdeutscher Verlag 1971

MAYNTZ, R.:
Die Implementation politischer Programme: Theoretische Über-
legungen zu einem neuen Forschungsgebiet.
Die Verwaltung 1977, S. 51-66

MILLER, G.A., GALANTER, E. and PRIBHAM, K.H.:
Strategien des Handelns.
Stuttgart: Klett 1973
Engl.: Plans and the Structure of Behavior. Holt, Rinehart
and Winston 1960

MOSER, H. und ORNAUER, H. (Hrsg.):
Internationale Aspekte der Aktionsforschung.
München: Kösel 1978

National Academy of Engineering, Committee on Public Engineering Policy: A Study of Technolgy Assessment.
Washington 1969

NEHNEVAJSA, J. and MENKES, J.:
Technology Assessment and Risk Analysis.
Unpublished Paper, National Science Foundation, October 1980

OECD:
Social Assessment of Technology - A Review of Selected Studies. Paris: OECD 1978

PASCHEN, H., BECHMANN, G., WINGERT, B.:
Funktion und Leistungsfähigkeit des Technology Assessment im
Rahmen der Technologiepolitik.
In: J.v. Kruedener und K.v. Schubert (Hrsg.): Technikfolgen
und sozialer Wandel. Köln: Verlag Wissenschaft und Politik
1981, 57-82

PASCHEN, H., GRESSER, K., CONRAD, F.:
Technology Assessment - Technologiefolgenabschätzung, Frank-
furt/New York: Campus 1978

PORTER, A. and ROSSINI, F.:
Evaluation Designs for Technolgy Assessments and Forecasts.
Technological Forecasting and Social Change 10 (1977),
369-380

PORTER, A.L., ROSSINI, F.A., CARPENTER, S.R. and ROPER, A.T.:
A Guidebook for Technology Assessment and Impact Analysis.
New York, Oxford: North Holland 1980

REESE, J., KUBICEK, H., LANGE, B.-P., LUTTERBECK, R.,
REESE, U.:
Bestandsaufnahme der Wirkungsforschung im Bereich Informa-
tionstechnologie. Ergebnisbericht.
Gesellschaft für Mathematik und Datenverarbeitung, Institut
für Planungs- und Entscheidungssysteme, Bonn 1978

SCHACHT, K.:
Sozialwissenschaftliche Begleitung als Planungsinstrument:
Das Beispiel Datenverarbeitung im Gesundheitswesen.
In: C. Böhret u.a. (Hrsg.), Planung in öffentlicher Hand.
Opladen 1977, S. 169-177

TRIBE, L.H.:
Technolgy Assessment and the fourth discontinuity: The limits
of instrumental rationality.
Southern California Law Review 46 (1973), 617-660

VOLPERT, W. (Hrsg.):
Beiträge zur Psychologischen Handlungstheorie.
Bern, Stuttgart, Wien: Huber 1980

WEISS, C.:
Evaluierungsforschung. Methoden zur Einschätzung von sozia-
len Reformprogrammen.
Opladen: Westdeutscher Verlag 1974
Engl.: Evaluation Research. Englewood Cliffs (N.H.), Pren-
tice-Hall 1972

WOLLMANN, H. und HELLSTERN, G.-M.:
Sozialwissenschaftliche Untersuchungsregeln und Wirkungs-
forschung - Zur Chance kritischer Sozialwissenschaft im Rah-
men staatlicher Forschungsaufträge.
In: P. Haugns (Hrsg.), Res Publica, Festschrift für D.
Sternberger, München 1977. S. 415-466

WYNNE, B.:
The rhetoric of consensus politics: A critical review of
technology assessment.
Research Policy 4 (1975), 108-158

Norbert Szyperski, Ursula M. Richter

A Constructive Approach for Impact Research on Information Technology

1. On the Assessment of Technological Impacts

Technological changes imply societal changes. These changes can only be considered positive and be called a technological progress if they are able to improve the degree of satisfaction of societal needs.

Technology assessment should help to estimate and evaluate the contribution of new technologies to social progress before their actual introduction, their new or their more widespread application. Doing technology assessment should provide better insights into the range and strength of negative as well as positve impacts. Though technology assessment cannot remove the uncertainties, however, it has the potential of reducing them.

Information technology shows a quite different set of problem dimensions in comparison to other technologies which have been or are going to be the subject of technology assessments.

Environmental changes have been identified as the crucial impact area of most of the technologies. Information technology, however, is supposed, on the one hand, to improve our ecological situation, but on the other hand, to bring about dangers for the individuality of persons and even to influence our cognitive style.

Never before there existed such a feeling of competition between human capabilities and technology. We accept technologies which extend our physical limitations but, as far as information technologies, as much as computers are concerned, we think that e.g. human beings have to be more intelligent and always superior to computers.

So the basic situation of information technology can be considered as being different from those of other technologies.

To remain in a position of seeing only the dangers information technology could mean to personality and society might be a dangerous position too. We need to understand the positive effects and the potential inherent in information technologies to solve current problems. Presently we do not fully comprehend the position of information technology within our society. Information Society is an often used term, but nobody is able to explain what it really means.

What can technology assessment bring about in such a situation? We can take the position of just trying to get a better understanding, more insights into the problems or we can try to identify the critical impact path of different technologies and contribute to the solution of related problems.

We would like to take the position of considering technology assessment as one dimension of our constructive work within society, necessary for developping our society in desired directions.

Then the question arises of how we should allocate our efforts. Performing technology assessment, particularly when it is intended to be of a more comprehensive nature, takes considerable resources. However, not in all cases of technology applications, assessment studies are really essential, but when they are necessary, the degree of accuracy can still vary over a wide range.

In Fig. 1 the different situations which have to be considered while deciding about technology assessment projects are represented.

Because of the extent to which technological changes are
able to impact societal needs in negative or positive terms,
it is reasonable to start with activities which could push,
stop or modify technological developments and their applications, and to alter other influencing factors which have the
potential to cause negative or positive effects. The necessity of such activities can in advance be recognized only in
some cases. On the other hand we can distinguish the cases
that activities are actually taken or omitted.

		Activities			
		necessary		not necessary	
		recognized	not recognized	recognized	not recognized
A c t i v i t i e s	are taken	1.1	1.2	1.3	1.4
	are not taken	2.1	2.2	2.3	2.4

Fig. 1: Matrix of possible constellations

In case 1.1 the situation is advantageous. TA is necessary to secure the choice of the right activity.

If activities are undertaken without having recognized their necessity (1.2), this is likely to result in a dangerous situation. Only under favourable conditions positive results can be achieved. This indicates that TA is essential to make sure that the right kinds of actions are taken.

In cases 1.3 and 1.4 the actions probably cause unconsidered effects. At least they are superfluous. TA could contribute to recognize such situations and to avoid disadvantageous actions.

If the necessity of activities is recognized but none are actually undertaken (2.1), then a good chance is missed. TA could be very useful in this case as well as under the condition that the urgency of activities is not realized (2.2) in order to make clear the requirements of planned action.

In the two remaining cases TA is not necessary and the decision not to undertake actions is appropriate.

The matrix clarifies the fact that the objectives and tasks of TA can vary to a considerable extent, thus their degree of detail and comprehensiveness is subject to variations depending on the prevailing conditions.

There remain a lot of other questions, such as in what situation we should try to do the assessment work. Should it be done in a very early stage when ideas about new technologies arise, should it go along with the development or construction of the technology or should it be done after its implementation?

In discussing all these questions, we have to be aware that there are certain limits inherent in assessments which cannot be overcome.

2. Immanent Limits of Assessments

Research on technological impacts can be seen as a planning instrument and as part of the planning process. Thus, limits of planning are valid for technology assessment. Four groups of arguments which outline systems immanent limits can be pointed out:

- the missing theory,
- the lack of appropriate instruments,
- the economy of assessments,
- the missing control of complexity[1].

The first three arguments are already well known in the TA discussion. So, only the last one shall be considered in more detail in this paper.

Tenbruck[2] tries to show the limits which planning activities have when they are directed towards living systems. He explains these limits implicit in the complexity of systems by

---

1) See Szyperski, N. und Welters, K., Grenzen und Zweckmäßigkeit der Planung. Eine Diskussion der Argumente aus betriebswirtschaftlicher Sicht. Arbeitsbericht Nr. 1 des Seminars für Allgemeine Betriebswirtschaftslehre und betriebswirtschaftliche Planung, Köln 1975.

2) See Tenbruck, F.H., Zur Kritik der planenden Vernunft, München 1972, 62 pp.

means of four factors. He argues that (1) knowledge does not
necessarily improve foresight, (2) agreement on a societal
goal system is hard to achieve, (3) need structures are
extremely unstable and (4) a changed reality implied by
technological applications can cause latent needs to be no
longer satisfied. Fig. 2 shows some of these interdependencies.

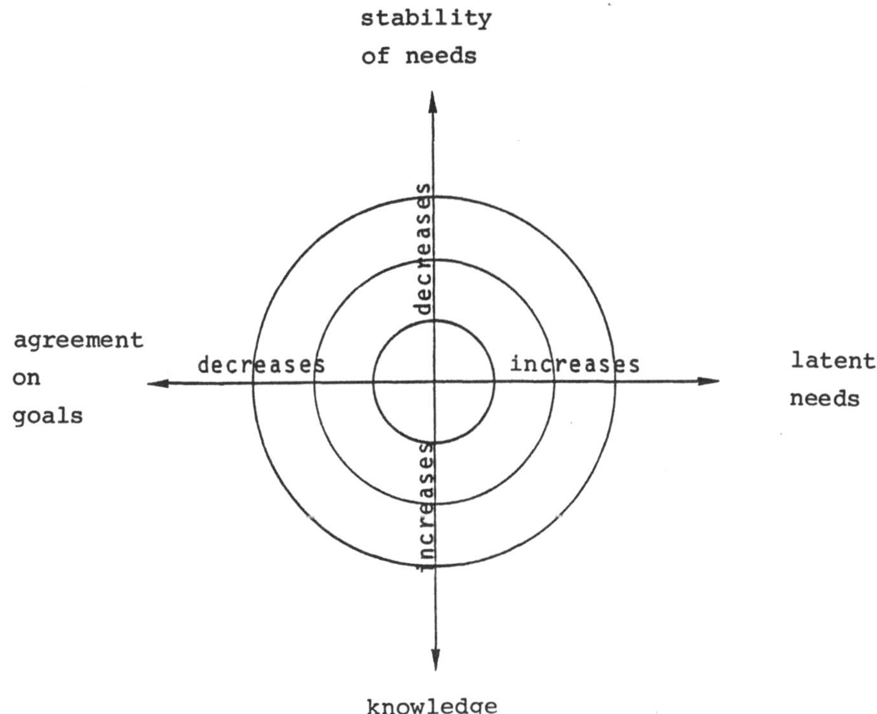

Fig. 2: Zones of decreasing assertion power

Let us first consider the dimension 'knowledge'. Increased
knowledge, which could be used for doing better forecasting,
is as well used for actions by the system in question. Adaptations and changes of the system will increase again and
again the incertainties of forecasting.

The second dimension of Tenbruck's goal system shows again a very crucial problem within technology assessment. If there is only one value- and goal-system, it is rather easy to do an assessment. But in our society there exist quite a variety of goal- and value-systems, which are often competing with each other. So the question arises whether there are as many assessments studies necessary as different value systems exist or which value system has to be used. What is the societal goal and value system?

Technological changes should be directed towards a better fulfillment of societal needs. But these needs are not stable, and technological changes also are leading to changes in the need structure. The same can be stated for technology assessment. So TA has to cope with this instability, but in turn it often contributes to instability itself.

Our need structure is not apparent. Often we believe that we do know our needs. But usually we just consider the needs which are not or not sufficiently enough satisfied. Changes evoking a better fulfillment of some of our apparent needs could therefore cause a worse fulfillment of latent needs so far satisfied. Here we encounter one of the main problems of TA. TA has to discover those latent needs probably endangered by technological changes. But as more latent needs exist, it becomes more difficult to discover them and to get good results out of TA.

In considering what TA can do for our society, these inherent limits have to be made conscious since expectations which are going beyond the implicit system restrictions are doomed to fail.

3. On the Notion of a Constructive Concept of Research on Impacts of Information Technology

Current approaches of research on impacts can be considered mainly descriptive. But there is further potential inherent in this research. It can contribute in a constructive way to technological progress. The objective of a constructive approach of research on impacts can therefore be summarized as follows:

> Research on impacts of technologies is intended
> to result in a constructive contribution to the
> efforts towards better fulfillment of societal
> needs.

Research on impacts should therefore not only elaborate consciousness towards possible dangers but should also be actively concerned with finding solutions. It can be seen as an active, constructive approach to adaptation processes of society to changing circumstances.

3.1. Strategic Attitudes Towards Technologies

As mentioned earlier the underlying societal goal- and value-system is of great importance for the outcome of a technology assessment study. Therefore it seems to be a useful approach not to start TA's by investigating a certain technology and questioning the pro's and con's, but to discuss and argue the strategic attitudes of the different individuals groups involved. In the past discussions with planning groups and decision makers within organisations made clear that this is a very helpful approach within enterprises.

In the fig. 3 four basic techno-strategic attitudes are differentiated.

	techno-strategic attitudes			
	defensive strategy	momentum strategy	moderate strategy	aggressive future-oriented strategy
scientist				
technician				

promoter
  . politician
  . producer
  . distributor
  . unions
  .				

persons affected
  . user
  . client
  .
  .				

A <u>defensive strategy</u> would mean trying to find a way back in order restore an earlier position of technological development.

Following the <u>momentum strategy</u> implies keeping up with technological innovations and to be open for technological changes, creating something like up a 'window to technology'.

An attitude of reserve is expressed in the <u>moderate strategy</u>. Taking this position one will ask for more information before technologies are actually applied. In this case research has a very important role. Tests, "Begleitforschung", i.e. pilot studies and social experiments have to be done to get more experience with the technologies in question.

To be a pioneer, a frontier man in technology, could be described as taking an <u>aggressive position</u>. The pioneer will easily take risks and get involved in new developments.

Each of these positions has its advantages and disadvantages. The important question mentioned by Mr. Reese for the point of no return is yet valid for all of these strategies. When the point of no return has been passed so that a system is irreversible, then, of course, it could be too late to start with pilot studies or to try to reverse from an undesired development by abandoning the technology in question.

3.2. Strategic Positions

The different interest groups in this technology game, scientists, technicians, the promotors, politicians, producers and so on, will take different positions. But what are the underlying reasons for taking a certain position. Can it be found in the respective personality, for example, to be a risk taking, or a more moderate personality, or are there other factors involved:

One reason could be seen in the results of a comparison with technological and economic positions of other countries. One could find e.g. his own position by looking at the availability of resources. So let us differentiate, for example, natural, financial, human and information resources.

In fig. 4 three different situations of available resources are represented.

Why could such a picture support taking an aggressive technology strategy? The welfare of a country is dependent on his resources. It will therefore aspire to improve its resource situation. But the allocation of natural resources is already well established, and they are increasable only to a very limited degree (e.g. better technologies for a better exploitation). Financial and human resources can only be influenced within a certain range. The resource which can

be best influenced is information. Especially for Germany,
which has almost no natural resources, there are well
founded reasons to build up information technology, despite
the fact that we can see not only chances but dangers too.

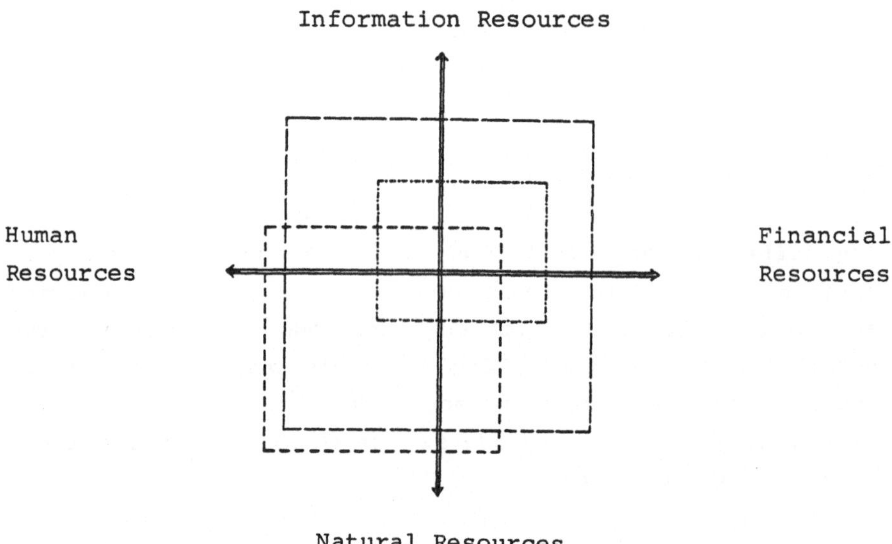

Fig. 4: Resource diagram

As to the strategic position the question often arises
whether a scientist, a TA-group should take a certain position at all.

Because of the complex nature of the problems under investigation, it does not seem to be possible to remain truly
neutral. Closely related to this point is the question
whether a TA group should function as something like an
attorney for a certain position or for a certain interest
group. If a position is taken, it has to be done in a very
explicit way and the limits implied by such positions have
to be seen very clearly.

3.3. Aspects of Constructivity in Research

The constructivity aspect expressed in the objective of TA has as well to be reflected in its actual research approach. This can be realized in various ways some of which are described briefly.

Considering the <u>utilization of the research results</u>, two points seem to be important:

- Using the research results as support for decisions, the results have to underline the positive or negative contributions of the technology or technology application in question together with corresponding alternatives which might have to be newly developed.
- The development of technologies and their applications cannot be seen as a process purely determined by technological features. The impacts and their evaluations are dependent on the occurence of a certain kind of combination of technical, social, political, economic up to ideological factors. The research results can point out the crucial influencing factors of certain impacts and can suggest modifications or new developments, even of non technical factors.

As far as the <u>research method</u> is concerned, constructive research on impacts implies its results to have a practical value. The <u>research strategy</u> can as well mean a more active role of the researcher in the process of development itself. As mentioned earlier, especially experiments are needed. New systems have to be set up and investigated. Research should go beyond 'Begleitforschung', it should be what is called 'research by development'.[1]

---

1) See Szyperski, N., Forschungsstrategien in der Angewandten Informatik - Konzepte und Erfahrungen -, In: Angewandte Informatik, Vol. 4 (1974), pp. 148 - 153.

Regarding the <u>subject of research</u>, the intention of constructive research in contributing to a better fulfillment of
societal needs results in the choice of subjects of concern
which cause essential changes in the need structure
(deteriorations or improvments). Here we again come across
the well known problem of avoiding the failure of the third
kind. Furthermore, the research subject, be it a technology,
a technology-related problem or objective, has to be of
relevance and actuality for society. It is important that
the research on impacts is undertaken in a stage of development when there are still options open for taking corrective
actions.

It is one of the underlying conditions of constructive
impact research that all interested parties are involved
in an active way (<u>research participants</u>). This implies as
well that the different goal systems of the parties involved
have to be considered and carefully taken into account.
Beyond that, the goal systems probably valid in the future,
when the impacts occur, have to be included too.

In this context it should be mentioned that there exists a
quite high degree of learning capability, responsiveness
and adaptability in the society, which should not be under-
estimated.

The ideas on constructive research can be well applied to
research of impacts of information technology. Information
technology is currently in a stage where important innovations or widespread applications are foreseeable for the
near future. But there does not exist any knowledge about
the effects of technology applications, whether they are
beneficial or deteriorative to the quality of life.

Horstfried Läpple

**Anticipating Future Use of Technology
- Factors Influencing Technology Transfer in General
and from Government R & D Agencies in Particular -**

This paper focuses on the question of how to improve the ability to identify, to evaluate and to set forth planned efforts for technology transfer. To anticipate the future use of technology is a task of vast scope and substantial complexity, because it is a process across established lines and is outside well understood patterns of technical application. In what follows is based on the assumption that a major improvement can be gained if there is a detailed knowledge of factors influencing technology transfer.

Technology transfer is not of interest for industry only. In some cases good reasons exist that government agencies perform R & D, in particular if the technology is characterized by high risk, long term, high social rate of return etc.. Therefore, factors influencing technology transfer in general and technology from government agencies to industry are described.

The analysis represented in this paper is based on contract work performed by the author at Stanford University for the National Aeronautics and Space Administration (Läpple, 1979).

1. Factors influencing technology transfer in general

In what follows, some factors are described which are important for evaluation of the application potential of technologies, for transfermechanism and for impacts of technologies on industry.

To check out the application potential of technologies the following factors are important:

o Most technologies have certain characteristics making them advantageous for some applications and useless for others. The application of numerical control in the machine tool industry is not economical for long production runs. Other factors like preparatory and maintenance work have to be taken into account, especially if skilled work force is scarce. One must also check the impacts of a technology on the organization of the whole production system. Often, a new technology - even if only a small piece - can only be used advantageously if the whole production system is re-organized. It is extremely difficult - if not impossible -to detail the general characteristics of technologies, due to the fact that production systems differ from indus-try to industry and even within a certain industry.

o Estimation of the relative efficiency of a new technology in comparison to already existing ones is an important fac-tor. Often, new technologies offer few or no advantages in terms of technical and cost aspects when compared to those already in use (see also: Cooper et al., 1973, p. 56). Sometimes engineers need a substantial amount of time to find out efficient ways to operate a new process. Further-more, there might be a defender (already existing techno-logy) and a challenger (new technology) situation. Estima-tion of the efficiency curves of old and new technologies and the 'switch-over-points' is an 'extremely hazardous task' (Wills, 1969, p. 5; see also: Ayres, Shapanka, Stern, 1975, p. 74). This situation delays the use of a techno-logy. The knowledge of this delay is of major interest due to the fact that the new technology might itself become ob-solete prior to implementation.

o In some cases one would fail in judging the value of a new technology without analyzing its 'neighbouring' technolo-gies. Often, efficient technologies cannot be used because "parallel necessary technology did not arise elsewhere" (Locke, 1978, p. 25). It takes time to make neighboring technologies available due to the fact that 6 to 10 years are often required to develop a process from pilot stage to industry scale.

o An extremely important factor is the development of technological innovation and the development of the diffusion
  process. It seems reasonable that industry will slow down
  the adoption of new technologies if the speed of innovations is high. This is based on the fact that firms face
  the danger of investing in 'soon-to-be-obsolete technology' (Rosenberg, 1976b, p. 534). While such a pattern might
  be characteristic for a lot of cases it does not hold for
  all. In the computer industry, important innovations are
  characterized by a diffusion time of 3 to 5 years; innovations of less importance are delivered to the market within 1 year. Firms must be heavily active in R & D in order
  to achieve a competitive position in the market (Dunn,
  1979, pp. 3-4).

o In almost all cases production technology is capitalintensive. If capital goods already in use are relatively new
  and have long life cycles, the long-run cost advantage of
  a new technology might be outweighed by short-term financial returns (Ray, 1969, p. 45). On the other hand, if a
  new technology is able to overcome bottlenecks in an existing production system and thereby offer incremental change
  compatible to the existing technology, it is likely that
  such a technology would be used immediately (See also:
  Rosenberg, 1976a, p. 125).

For assessing transferpossibilities and transferrestric-
tions the factors mentioned below are of interest:

o Technical and business alignment between industries is of
  critical importance. In such cases it is not a question of
  technological availability but of wether the technology is
  known to all potential users. A certain technology might

be well known; a special technique might be general knowledge in one industry, but there is no way to know if this
knowledge is available to other industries as well. Vertical technology transfer, a process within one industry,
works quite well. In contrast, no established mechanisms
for horizontal technology transfer exist, a process which
takes place across organizational borders.

o Interdisciplinary barriers exist due to the fact that each
field in science and technology has developed its own channels and has created an individual methodology for problem
solving. How difficult it is to overcome interdisciplinary
barriers can be assessed by analyzing fields with interdisciplinary character. One example is Operations Research.
In the American Journal of Operations Research it is estimated that about 10 % of the published articles are of interest for a special target group but actually only 2 % to
4 % reach this target group due to language barriers
(Pierskalla, 1979, p. 8).

o A major influence from regulations is expected if implemented in the form of so-called design characteristics. A
firm may feel it is inconvenient to try to change governmental rules for the benefit of a minor improvement and
thereby will not use a technology which only leads to moderate benefits.

To evaluate the impacts of new technology on industry the
following factors have to be taken into account:

o New technologies are both market-creating and market-destroying. Market-destroying effects will be greater the
more existing technology is integrated into the production
system. It is important to realize that it is insufficient
to assess those effects at the firm level only. For example,

replacement of pesticides might impact the cosmetics industry because both industries use common raw materials. Attempts of oil companies to achieve control over competitive uranium and coal technologies "may be seen as attempts to assure long term market control by minimizing the potential threats arising from technological breakthroughs in the provision of substitute products" (Rosenberg, 1976b, p. 533). Another recent example is the behavior of the electric utilities towards solar power due to the fact that such a decentralized energy source does not fit the structure of existing centralized power line networks (Commoner, 1979, pp. 69 - 71). Those examples clearly show that the market-destroying effects of a technology may lead to the non-application of a new technology or at least to a delay in the diffusion process.

o Another case to consider is a major change of the production technology in an entire industry branch. If one firm goes ahead it will face tremendous risk. Other firms, choosing the 'second fast' strategy, would gain the technical knowledge by monitoring the research work of the innovator (Thurow, 1978, p. 70). They will follow if it is economical to do so. The first firm may not gain substantial comparative advantage.

o Dependent on its stage of development, a firm shows different responsiveness to different kinds of innovations. Utterback (1976, p. 36) offers the following explanation:

During the first stage, development is based on product change primarily. Consequently, product innovations have priority over process innovations. Based upon experiences, e.g. in the semi-conducter industry, firms concentrating on process innovations in this early stage face the danger of improving the production technology of a product which soon might become obsolete.

The second stage finds established firms in an industry looking for process innovations. Small changes, compatible with the existing production system, reduce costs of existing products.

In the third stage, established firms might have incentives to delay major technological changes because of the inflexibility of capitalintensive production systems.

It is important to realize that such a life cycle is not a one-way street. Rather there might be a switch from aging back to growth due to technological change and or changes in the social setting.

2. Factors influencing technology transfer from a government R & D agency to industry

The factors analyzed in the following are of particular interest if a governmental R & D agency is challenged in providing for the widest practicable and appropriate use of its R & D activities.

o For successful introduction of a new technology the relation between innovation and innovator is most important. Many firms have adopted a procedure assuring that the person who made the innovation will become the product manager for the concerned product later on. In almost all cases of government performed R & D there is a separation of the innovator from the innovation, there is a highly fragmented process which is supposed to have a negative impact on technological innovation. This assumption is supported by empirical investigations (e.g.: Chakrabarti, 1972, p. 28; Baer et al., 1976, p. 48). The less different organizations are involved in the delivery process of a new technology from conceptualization to the introduction in the market the more likely it is that a new product will reach the market and more likely it is that the delivery process is speed up (Yin, 1978, p. 13).

o It is important to realize that the technology is not born in a commercial environment. There is a trend, like in the military field, to produce technologies as soon as it is technically feasible. But technical feasibility is no guarantee for commercial success. Of course, a lot of fine examples exist like integrated circuits, supersonic airplane etc. But there are also other ones like the nuclear driven ship. It is possible that the relaxation of the profitability constraint leads to earlier applications of a technology. If it is commercial to use the technology, substantial technical knowledge is already existent and a much more faster utilization can take place. But no one knows when and if at all it is useful to use such a technology.

o Concern about competition between government agencies and industry is frequently mentioned. It is claimed that to some extent national laboratories engage in "research on technology of commercial significance and thereby directly compete with private industry" (Hollomon, 1979, p. 39). This argument has to be taken very seriously because it is likely that in such cases private activities will be eliminated for ever.

o Psychological barriers to the use of government information and technology and, to some extent the restricted availability of government produced technologies are important. There is - justified or not - industry's concern that government would try to influence its activities or at least monitor the requests. The hesitation of industry to employ government R & D products is also caused by the often overemphasized role and publicity concerning government R & D agencies.

o Value of externally generated information about technologies in general has to be taken into account. Many firms believe that externally generated knowledge, when compared to its own R & D is not as unique as is often claimed (see also: VDI, 1979, p. 18). As a result, the value of a certain government R & D information is known to a firm only after a check of its content; that is to say after the firm has invested time and money (Johnson et al., 1977, p. 11).

o An important factor is that government R & D agencies by their own means might not be able to explore industry's needs. As mentioned before, new technologies are both market-creating and market-destroying. Such patterns are extremely difficult to assess without specific knowledge about industry. Without such detailed knowledge government R & D agencies face the danger of disseminating information which will not be used and to produce prototypes which will not be applied. One should keep in mind that in the U.S. in 1979 there are already some 30,000 government owned patents that have never been used.

The factors discussed above are only a few out of a large set. It was not intended to provide a complete list. An attempt was made to demonstrate that government R & D agencies face specific difficulties in promoting technology transfer, difficulties which add up to those confronting technology transfer in general.

Conclusions

The discussion of the previous subsections has shown how difficult it is to determine which factors influence technology transfer and in which way. Furthermore, the underlying cause-effect relations are not constant but changing in time and difficult to anticipate. These patterns are probably the main reason that the vast number of empirical studies on technology transfer have provided only a limited value for the formulation of effective policies.

One should be very carefully in operating with so-called principles like for example 'technology push' or 'demand pull'. Most empirical studies point out a clear preference for the demand pull policy. An investigation performed by Mowery and Rosenberg (1979) provides an in-depth analysis of eight of the most known empirical studies on technological innovation which all support the demand pull policy. The authors claim that "the role of demand has been overextended and misrepresented, with serious consequences for our understanding of the innovative process and of appropriate government policy alternatives to foster innovation " (Mowery, Rosenberg, 1979, p. 3).

Even if it is possible to gain complete understanding of a certain case - which might be possible very rarely only - a policy upon this case cannot be built.

References

Baer, Walter S. et al. (1976): Analysis of Federally Funded Demonstration Projects: Final Report, prepared for the Experimental Technology Incentives Program, U.S. Department of Commerce, The Rand Corporation, Report R-1926-DOC, April 1976

Chakrabarti, Alok K. (1972): The Effects of Techno-Economic and Organizational Factors on the Adoption of NASA-Innovations, Ph.D. Thesis, Northwestern University

Commoner, Barry (1979): The Politics of Energy, New York

Cooper et al. (1973): Strategic responses to technological threats, in: T.B. Green and F.R. Dennis (Eds.), Academy of Management Proceedings, 33rd Annual Meeting, Boston, Mass., Aug. 19-22, pp. 54-59

Dunn, Donald A. (1979): Organizational Options for the transfer of space technology to commercial markets, Feb., Program in Information Policy, Engineering-Economic Systems Department, Stanford University

Hollomon, Herbert J. (1979): Government and the innovation process, in: Technology Review, Vol. 81, No. 6, pp. 30-41

Johnson, Douglas F. et al., (1977): NASA Tech Brief Program: A Cost Benefit Evaluation, prepared for Office of Industry Affairs and Technology Utilization, National Aeronautics and Space Administration, Washington, D.C., Contract NASW-2892

Läpple, Horstfried (1979): Improving NASA's Technology Trans-
    fer Process through increased screening and evaluation
    in the Information Dissemination Program, Engineering-
    Economic Systems Department, Stanford University, Report
    No. 28, National Aeronautics and Space Administration,
    Contract NASW 3204

Locke, Brian H. (1978): Planning Innovation, in: Long Range
    Planning, Vol. II, No. 6, Dec., pp. 21-29

Mowery, David and Rosenberg, Nathan (1978): The influence of
    market demand upon innovation; a critical review of some
    recent empirical studies, Stanford University

Pierskalla, William P. (1979): An open letter to authors, in:
    OR/MS Today, Operations Research/Management Science, Vol.
    6, No. 2, p. 8

Ray, G. F. (1969): The diffusion of new technology, a study
    of ten processes in nine industries, National Economic
    Review, No. 48, pp. 40-100

Rosenberg Nathan (1976a): Perspectives on technology, Cam-
    bridge

Rosenberg Nathan (1976b): On technological expectations, The
    Economic Journal, 86, pp. 523 - 535

Stern, M.O., Ayres R.U. and A. Shapanka (1975): A model for
    forecasting the substitution of the technology for another,
    in: Technological Forecasting and Social Change, Vol. 7,
    pp. 57 - 79

Thurow, Lester C. (1978): Eight imperatives for R & D, Tech-
    nological Review, Vol. 80, No. 3, pp. 64 - 70

Utterback, James M. (1976): The dynamics of technological behaviour, in: Has the U.S. lost the initiative? Proceedings on a Symposium on Technological Innovation, Washington D.C., April 19 - 20, 1976

Verein Deutscher Ingenieure (1979): Transferhilfe für Erfindungen, ein System zur weiten Verbreitung technischer Ideen, VDI-Nachrichten, Nr. 16, 20. April, p. 18

Wills, G. (1969): The Art and Management of Technological Forecasting, in: Wills (Ed): Technological Forecasting, London, pp. 3 - 16

Yin, Robert K. (1978): Contemporary issues in domestic technology transfer, in: Domestic Technology Transfer: Issues and Options, prepared by the Subcommittee on Science, Research and Technology, U.S. House of Representatives, Ninety-Fifth Congress, Second Session, Vol. I, pp. 3 - 39

Niels Bjørn-Andersen

Public Participation in Technology Assessment

A researcher is not a special kind of man
but every man is a special kind of researcher
C. West Churchman

Introduction

The problem of public participation is urgent. On a growing
number of issues today large groups are publicly voicing
concern about a vast array of technological advances ranging
from the Concorde, nuclear power, new life forms created via
bioengineering, to information technology. To an increasing
extent grassroots movements demand insight into the research
and development processes as well as thorough assessment of
the consequences of all the new major technologies.

As these demands are seldom met, conflicts between parts of
the public and those authorities which commissioned the technology accelerates and confrontations get more violent, e.g.
public demonstrations at sites proposed for nuclear power
plants or at the new Japanese airport. Larger sectors of the
public are beginning to doubt the right of the authorities
to protest, break up demonstrations, etc. Researchers like
Mathiesen and Christie, highly esteemed Norwegian professors,
have even spoken about the necessity of "civil disobedience"
when the interests of a small group are threatened by the
majority in a democratic state. Similarly, the notion of
"civil disobedience" has taken on greater significance and
acquired new dimensions in the u.S. As a Danish philosopher,
Henningsen, once said, "A democracy is characterized by the
way in which it treats its minorities."

One way to approach this problem, which has sometimes been
called a crisis in our democracy, is to ask for more democratic
control of the development and the application of technologies.
This would, in a sense, broaden the debate, require a clearer
articulation of the full range of costs and benefits, and involve the participation of not only technical experts but the
affected at large.

Im am very grateful to Ida R. Hoos for constructive criticism
and a very careful editing of the language.

The question is how to establish this control so as to achieve public input into technology assessment. Most manifestations to date have been the activities of organized interest groups/ organizations (automobile associations, consumer associations, association against the use of nuclear power, trade unions, etc.). On occasion, there has been participation - generally via opposition - by some spontaneous grassroots groups, such as local citizens against a new road, employees against a new computer system, or environmentalists against a new power plant. In these cases "the public" has demanded a right to take part in technology assessment and thus in the politics of the decision-making.

This paper will address the question, how "the public" might participate in the kind of impact that must enter into a proper technology assessment, assuming at least for the moment that we agree on what constitutes the <u>public</u> and what constitutes <u>research</u>. As we shall see, it is not all that clearcut.

Can the public participate in technology assessment?

The answer is obviously no, if we take a traditional view. A Danish professor of computer science expressed it recently:

> "I am tired of the technology debate today. An
> intellectual elite is dominating. All the time
> they demand to control technology. They want to
> take part in the programming, which is difficult
> even for us specialists. In my opinion, they
> should leave research to specialists."
> (Bjørner 1981)

I can agree that the public should not take part in the programming. But this is not to say that the public should not take part in the decisions about what to program, whether to invest in major efforts to introduce television satellites,

or whether to have nuclear power or conventional power - especially with respect to the different types of risks associated
with each of the two types of technologies. What I am saying
is not that "the public" must always participate. What I am
saying is that the individuals who must live with the consequences - especially the negative ones - should have the
right and opportunity to express their concerns and formulate
their own demands as part of the decision.

A second issue relates to the question about what we understand by participation. Blumberg (1972) cites the following
degrees of participation (slightly modified):

I   Co-operation
    1. Right to get information
    2. Right to protest
    3. Right to put forward suggestions
    4. Right to negotiate before the
       decision is made by the authority

II Co-determination
    1. Right to veto
       a) temporarily, postponing the decision
          for a certain period
       b) temporarily, postponing the decision
          until there have been negotiations,
       c) permanently

    2. Joint decision-making, where both or all
       parties have to agree

    3. Decision right alone, complete autonomy within
       that particular area.

It is quite obvious that the degree of influence increases
as one moves down the list. However, even the concept of

influence is elusive as one has to be aware of structural power, i.e. the power imbedded in the norms, values, and procedures that one "normally" follows (Lukes 1978, Christensen & Daugard 1980).

The point should be made that it is not possible, necessary, nor desirable to involve the "man in the street" in every decision. We cannot ask whether he wants a relational data base with advanced information retrieval facilities containing all available information. At worst he will specify the colour of the data base, at best he will punch the nose of the person asking. Why, how, and to what extent people can or wish to be involved in the assessment process reflect an enormous, complicated, kaleidoscopic configuration of factors personal, philosophical, political, psychological, and economic. Understandably the dynamics of the participation process calls upon the full range of behavioural and social sciences.

A given individual cannot possibly take an informed stand on every technological innovation and he may not care to.

This is a fact of life that has bearing on the research methodologies we use in technology assessment. The author has carried out several studies, using different methodologies, of the impact of computer systems in banks. Although the computer applications did exhibit some differences, they were, seen from our distant vantage point, fairly similar. In spite of this the results of the studies were a clear reflection of the research methodologies used. In one study, we used postal questionnaires (Bjørn-Andersen & Jappe 1979); in a second, we used intensive interviews (Bjørn-Andersen et al. 1979); in the third, we used task groups of employees to conduct a series of meetings after they had been exposed to a one-week course (Clausen 1981). The main difference in

the evaluations of the computer system in these three studies
was that the employees got more critical when they had an
opportunity to develop their own framework for understanding
the situation and for diagnosing the changes introduced by
the computer system. Furthermore, it is noteworthy that the
employees got more interested in actually participating in
designing their own work environment in relation to the
computer system.

The same holds true of the public at large. It is impossible
to participate in research on technology assessment unless
one has devoted some time to it, has acquired some knowledge,
has some support from others of the same opinion, and has
some power through a democratic procedure. I shall deal with
these issues in the next section.

Prerequisites of public participation in technology assessment

When we look to our traditional positivistic research methods
it becomes quite clear that these leave litte scope for the
man in the street to indulge in what we traditionally call
research. However, recalling the words by Churchman[1] we
realize that there is a need for a broader definition of
research if we are to bring in the ideas, wishes, and requests of the general public into technology assessment. To
do this we must shift the research paradigm. Researchers in
their ivory towers will have great difficulty in analyzing
consequences of technologies for the various affected; the
only remedy is to replace, at least in part, the positivistic-
oriented research by action-oriented research[2].

---

1) C.W. Churchman: "A researcher is not a special kind of man,
   but every man is a special kind of researcher."
2) Abnor & Bjerke, 1977; Hildebrand 1981; Johnsen 1979;
   Mathiesen 1973; Maløe 1979, and Sandberg 1975.

The changed research paradigm which I propose for research into an assessment of information technologies, has the following four clusters of prerequisites: structural conditions, actor conditions, methodological conditions, and technological conditions.

The <u>structural conditions</u> are probably the most important. If an individual by himself feels alienated because of the introduction of a new technology, his chances of actual participation in research on evaluating the consequences are slim if not non-existent. He must organize. He must join with others who share the same basic beliefs and attitudes and who are united in the wish to gain knowledge and actually influence the decisions. Therefore, it is necessary to organize in some way, perhaps in well established trade unions or consumer associations, or in spontaneous grassroots movements. Only if the individual takes part in some kind of interest organization will he stand a chance of getting some influence over research. If the individual acts alone, without any support group, he may come out even weaker than before (Mulder 1972). Furthermore, it is necessary to have legal sanctions for participation in the research. Trade unions in the Scandinavian countries have the right to participate in the design and implementation of new information technologies either by law (Sweden) or by agreement (Denmark und Norway). While these agreements do not automatically guarantee participation, they do give the right to demand it. Similarly, in regard to societal issues there are certain associations and organizations that have the right to demand information and to be heard before technological innovations occur. These organizations/associations have a responsibility for protecting the public interests.

In the actor-oriented conditions, education plays the major role. Thus almost all actor-oriented research has an element of education. In traditional action research one often talks

about "transfer of competence" from the researcher to the
members of the public actually participating. As Freire (1972)
among others pointed out in his critique of the banking
concept of education, no-one can educate another but everyone
can learn. Researchers should not proceed on the assumption
that they are going to tell the public what framework to
use, what analysis to employ, or even what kind of problem
to attack. These issues must be developed jointly by the
researcher and those who will be affected. Both must be prepared to learn and to transcend existing limitations.

The more affected (and oppressed) one is, the more important
it is to take as a starting point the situation of the individual. When evaluating new technology one needs facts, but
it is astonishing how few may be required in order to proceed.

In projects with a fairly limited scope, such as one concerned
with technology assessment of word processing in local authorities, we found that a three-day course was adequate for
choosing among certain types of word processors and for evaluating the benefits to the individuals and the organization
(Bjørn-Andersen & Skousen 1980). As Simon (1977) so aptly
puts it, "We do not have to be champion boxers to referee
a fight". The amount of factual knowledge need not be extreme,
for in using experts and counter experts, we can require
that they disclose how they reached their conclusions, what
reasoning they employed, what evidence they relied upon,
and what assumptions they made. Our decisions would then
be based on a logical analysis[1)2)].

More important than "facts" is the factor of self reliance.
Often oppressed groups will defend their lack of initiative

---

1) cf for example Mitroff's assumptional analysis (1980).
2) It may be noted that the learning process can be facilitated by use of means other than the written word, e.g.
   specific experiences, video films, small scale models, etc.

by stating that they know too little, they are too few, it has never worked before, etc. It is important that individuals understand that they can exert an influence through participation in the technology assessment process. This is not mere conjecture. Many different groups of the public have actually been able to participate meaningfully in technology assessment research. There are at present many examples, from a group of secretaries in an English chemical company planning their own work organization around two word processors to large-scale manifestations of protest regarding nuclear power.

Methodological conditions represent the third group in the new research paradigm. Most existing methods for designing information systems or for carrying out research projects - both having much in common - take as a starting point some kind of pre-defined objectives. They define the problem to be attacked, break it down into sub-problems, and perform logical analyses within these boundaries. These methods do not afford the general public the opportunity to take an active and decisive role in research projects. Four alternatives are suggested:

1. Instead of reducing and narrowing the problem, it is mandatory that the problem first be expanded. If we fail to do this, we find ourselves generating the most sophisticated solution to the wrong problem. When problem definition is the task of management or the systems specialist, user interests are poorly reflected or even excluded. This is understandable since "objective" systems evaluations conducted by experts reflect their own Weltanschauung and not that of the end-users or of persons affected by the systems. This is not to say that experts have no role to play, but merely to point out that they can be of considerable assistance to end-users in the course of their evaluation. Perhaps the emphasis should be on generalized, rather than on

specialized, knowledge, with <u>understanding</u> the first order of business. The business of design would come later.

2. One has to work <u>dialectically</u>. This means that in evaluating systems and in controlling the effects of new technological developments, conflicts are useful. Made more explicit and amplified, differences can help. Only then is there a chance of approaching the ideal of analyzing a reasonable spread of alternatives. If, on the contrary, this is not done, there is the danger of having alternatives which differ only marginally from oneanother while important aspects are excluded. This means that we have to design for deadly enemies (Churchman 1976), i.e. design an alternative which is the direct opposite (morphologically different) of the alternative proposed.

3. In order to get a proper perspective, an important part must be the <u>historical analysis</u>. This means that we have to work with dynamic rather than static models and in this way see each new technology or each new system as only one step in a long sequence of technological developments. This is especially important when considering information systems for they represent indirect technology. This means that it has no value in itself. The value of this technology is only in its application of controlling and monitoring other processes. Therefore it bears little resemblance to a technology like nuclear power which might be assessed at a particular point in time. Information technology must be assessed in a multitude of different contexts and over a longer time interval. Only then can we get to grips with statements like "microelectronics representing the second industrial revolution" or "microelectronics play an important part in the third wave" (Toffler 1981).

4. If we want to control technological developments, we must focus on <u>function</u> instead of <u>structure.</u> This means that we have to focus on the external properties of a system and its interaction with the environment instead of focussing on the programming language, the operating system, etc. If we want to assess a car we shall not go into how it is built but assess its relative impact on other systems, i.e. the transport function, pollution function, etc. and leave it to experts to tell why the car pollutes.

Finally, the fourth set is one of <u>"technological conditions"</u>. Our including it in the research paradigm is in itself a manifestation of the dialectics. In order to evaluate one technology, one has to use another. What we have found out, however, is that the attempts to use information technology to enhance information systems capabilities to assist the general public in participation efforts have fallen through.

At least two types have been tried out. One type is the "community memory" often provided by libraries where the general public could come and simply use the terminal for whatever purpose including that of information retrieval in library systems. Most of these systems have been abandoned as they were not used. Another example is the "information exchange" systems which give any group the chance to put anything on file for other groups to use. This should facilitate exchange of information between grassroots groups, but this too never seemed to catch on among these groups.

In our opinion participation by the "man-in-the-street" may be facilitated, if the right type of technology is applied. E.g. very few will refuse using a typewriter or a telephone as means of communication. In the same way other technological applications could be beneficial in the assessment of new technologies. However, the human being must be in control.

He must be able to understand the limitations and the relative advantages. The benefit of being able to communicate with many people on the phone using the sense of hearing may be obtained only by sacrificing face-to-face communication with a much smaller group where all senses could come into use. Accordingly, different technological possibilities could be used to facilitate participation in assessment. E.g. video-film used by the affected themselves or by their experts have proved very useful as shown by Enid Mumford, Manchester Business School.

A word of caution

Even when all the prerequisites mentioned above are met, there are still left unresolved many questions regarding the morality of the decision-making mode. In the case of information tech-nology we may need to evolve a new ethic. We have already observed the extent to which information technology has become a potent weapon in public opinion formation. That information is a tool for good or evil is a truism. We see today how interest groups, especially the better established ones, use information technology for furthering their cause. How then can we be certain that human values will be served to the ultimate benefit of mankind? Ellul has described a new ethic built on the following principles:

> Non-power (a concept parallel to the conviviality concept used by Illich) meaning that we must from time to time choose not to do things which we might have done. "We must choose the non-intercention each time there is uncertainty about the global and long-term effects of whatever actions are to be undertaken."

<u>Freedom</u>. We must realize that technology does not liberate us, as it did our ancestors. We have to liberate ourselves from technology, which is tying us down, in order to again become human beings ("he who ties a slave to himself also ties himself to a slave").

<u>Conflict</u>. Our ethics must accept conflicts. Technology demands standardisation, formalisation, averages and congruent action. Social systems on the other hand may function in constant interaction with conflicts and negotiations.

<u>Transgression and profanation</u>. Technology must be demythologized and Ellul suggests that "we must destroy the illusion of progress, the illusion that technique leads us from one achievement to another, the deep-rooted illusion that the material and the spiritual coincide."

These points made by Ellul are strongly supported by Cooley (1980) and Illich (1973) who talks about "Technology expropriating the tacit knowledge inherited through generations."

In a society where technology plays an ever increasing role and leaves the individuals virtually dependent on it, there is an obvious need for reflections on the extent to which these technologies contribute to a more human society. As Illich (1973) points out, we have reached, with regard to some technologies, the turning point where we have become totally dependent on these technologies. If we are to liberate ourselves it is mandatory to assess the dependencies of these technologies. And this should not be experts giving their wisdom from their ivory tower, but the assessment should emanate from the man-in-the-street, grassroots, employees, etc.

List of references

Ingeman Abnor & Bjørn Bjerke: Företagsekonomisk Metodläre, Lund 1977.

Niels Bjørn-Andersen & Bo Hedberg: Designing Information Systems in an Organisational Perspective, TIMS Studies, vol 5, 1977.

Niels Bjørn-Andersen, Bo Hedberg, Dorothy Mercer, Enid Mumford & Andreu Solé: The Impact of Systems Change in Organizations, The Netherlands, 1979.

Niels Bjørn-Andersen & Lone Jappe: Computer Impact and the Demand for Participation. In A. Niemi: A Link Between Science and Application of Automatic Control, Oxford, 1979.

Niels Bjørn-Andersen & Thomas Skousen: A Strategy for User Control of the Systems Development. A case of local government, Information Systems Research Group, Copenhagen, 1980.

Dines Bjørner: Angsten for ny teknologi skyldes uvidenhed, AC-Debat no. 4, April 1981.

Paul Blumberg: Arbejdspladsens demokrati, Copenhagen, 1972.

Søren Christensen & Poul Erik Daugard: Magt og deltagelse, Copenhagen, 1980.

C. West Churchman: The Design of Enquiring Systems, N.Y., 1971.

Hasse Clausen: Demokratisering og humanisering af systemarbejdet, Copenhagen, 1981.

Mike Cooley: Architect or Bee, Slough, 1980.

Jacques Ellul: The Power of Technique and the Ethics of Non-power.

Paulo Freire: The Pedagogy of the Oppressed, London, 1972.

Steen Hildebrandt: Videnskabsteoretiske betragtninger omkring erhvervsøkonomien, Erhvervsøkonomisk Tidsskrift, no. 1, 1981.

Ivan Illich: Tools for Conviviality, London, 1973.

Steven Lukes: Power, a Radical View, London, 1974.

Thomas Mathiesen: Det ufaerdige. Bidrag til politisk aktions-
    teori, Copenhagen, 1973.

Ian Mitroff: Toward a Logic and Methodology for Real-World
    Problems, In Niels Bjørn-Andersen (ed.): The Human Side
    of Information Processing, The Netherlands, 1980.

Mauk Mulder: Power Equalization through Participation?
    Administrative Science Quarterly, vol 16, no 1, March
    1971.

Erik Maløe: Aktør og aktionsforskning. Om medleven, forstaelse
    og tolkning, Aarhus, 1979.

Ake Sandberg: En fraga om metod, Stockholm 1975.

Herbert Simon: New Science of Management Decision Making,
    N.Y., 1977.

Alvin Toffler: The Third Wave, London, 1981.

Joseph Weizenbaum: Computer Power and Human Reason, N.Y.,
    1975.

Riccardo Petrella

The Practice of Project Choice and Assessment

The FAST Programme

<u>INTRODUCTORY REMARKS</u>

I was asked to answer three main questions:

(a) how the research programme was designed and its priority
    subject areas identified (FAST is focused on three main
    subject areas: work and employment, information society,
    "bio-society")[1].

(b) the criteria and procedures for the choice of the specific
    topics within the three main subject areas in addition to
    in-house work (FAST includes 30 research projects carried
    out by external contractors).

(c) how the research work and its results were evaluated and
    assessed.

The research programme being still under execution (most of
the projects will be completed by the beginning of 1982), I
shall only deal with (a) and (b).

The paper is divided into four section:

- in the <u>first section</u> I shall briefly introduce the contextual features of the FAST programme, i.e. a policy-oriented
  programme, a multi-actors exercise, etc.). They have significantly influenced the type and the modality of the programme design and projects choice.

- in the <u>second section</u>, issues specifically related to (a)
  will be addressed.

- issues related to (b) will be considered in the <u>third
  section</u>

- some concluding remarks will be made in the <u>fourth and last section</u>.

I. <u>THE RELEVANCE OF THE CONTEXTUAL FEATURES</u>

1. The following features are worth mentioning:

   - the demand for research was originated within and by a governmental body (the Council of Ministers of the European Community following a proposal by the Commission of the E.C.)

   - the research work is institutionally located inside the organisation that generated the demand (i.e. the research supplier and clients are part of the same organisation though there are some additional external clients)

   - the research programme is, by its very nature, a multi-actors exercise.

   - FAST is a pilot experiment limited in time, a first one of his kind at Community level.

2. A specific research need felt by a governmental institution was at the origin of the FAST programme (why, what, how).

   Its main mandate is to contribute to the elaboration of a coherent long term science and technology policy at Community level by the identification of priorities and options in the field of R-D, based on the assessment of the opportunities, problems and conflicts which are likely to affect the long term development of the Community.

FAST is not an exercise for theory validation or application. It has, however, an implicit function of methodological testing.

3. Similarly to research units established within governmental departments in some European countries (the SARU in the Department of Environment in the U.K.; la Division des Etudes Prospectives in the Ministry of Industries in France), FAST is an operational unit ("division") of the Directorate General for Science, Research and Development of the Commission of the E.C.. Formally located within the Commission services according to a vertical attribute, FAST deals, however, with horizontal issues.

This potential source of difficulties has not had any significant impact so far. From the very beginning of its existence, FAST has favoured a direct involvment into its work of the other concerned services in the Commission both formally and informally.

Because of its institutional location FAST activities (as research supplier) take place in a complex system where the final direct clients (the Commission and the Council of Ministers of the E.C.) are the system's top decision-makers.

Interesting enough, the final direct clients of FAST are not only two Community institutions. Because FAST is to report to the Council of Ministers, via the Commission, it also reports de facto to the concerned departments of the national governments.

4. FAST is multi-actors exercise

   - as a unit within a hierarchical structure (a Directorate
     General)

   - being under the responsibility and "guidance" (via the
     Directorate General) of a member of the Commission

   - the Commission is its first main client: the Commission
     made the proposals to the Council for the launching of
     the programme; it has to evaluate the results of FAST
     and transmit them to the Council

   - the Council of Ministers is the final main client while
     governmental departments of member States play indivi-
     dually and collectively (via CREST)[2] a continuous role
     of filters/controllers/evaluators.

FAST has institutional co-partners: all the other commission services directly concerned by FAST projects (in
practice, the vast majority of the existing Directorates
General).
As any Community research programme belonging to the category called "indirect action" (i.e. the funding of the
research projects under contract is shared by the Community and the member States), FAST has an <u>Advisory Committee
on Programme Management</u> (ACPM). The ACPM, composed of external personalities (24) appointed by the member States,
has a consultative role. They are directly involved in any
major decision concerning the life of the programme, from
its start to its end.

These co-sponsors are additional "clients" furthermore,
since FAST's 30 research projects under contract are co-
financed by various organisms (often ministries) from the
member States, the work programme had to be submitted for

information and reaction to the <u>Committee for Energy and Research of the European Parliament</u>. The Parliament will have to be consulted by the Council of Ministers on the result of FAST programme.

The list of clients ends with a last but not least category: the scientific community at large. Though the "other researchers" are not FAST direct clients, they are of decisive importance as they will be the channels through which FAST scientific credibility will be assessed during the evaluation phase of the FAST results by the member States.[3]

Finally, the programme involves two main research actors:
. the team itself (6 researchers, 4 support staff)
. the research centres working under contract (there are 49) within the 30 research projects.

II. <u>THE DEFINITION OF THE RESEARCH DESIGN</u>

1. In section 1 we pointed out that the <u>why</u> of the research programme was given[4].

To a large extent, the same applied to the <u>what</u>. In fact, the mandate of the Council of Ministers specified that work should be concentrated on the following <u>three priority areas</u>

- long-term supply of resources
- long-term technical and structural change
- long-term social change.

In view of <u>the very high level of abstraction</u> of the content definition of the three priority areas, the first task of the FAST team was (a) to outline in a more precise way the overall concept of the programme without departing from the Council of Ministers terms of reference and (b) on this basis, to specify the scope and content of the main priority subject areas. The definition stage took approximately 6 months. It directly involved, in addition to the FAST team

- the other concerned services of the Commission
- the members of the ACPM.

2. To accomplish this task, the FAST team

- carried out a broad analysis of the major changes likely to affect the long-term development of European societies. The results were integrated in a report L'Europe en mutation[5]

- designed a procedure for the selection and definition of the most critical, long-term problems-areas for the Community.

3. To this end we proceeded as it follows:

- First we made an assessment of the general goals and objectives of the European Community as they were emerging on the top of more often and explicitely declared Community targets (material prosperity of member countries: 9 priorities; internal Community stability and cohesion: 6 priorities; societal justice and freedom: 4 priorities; environmental integrity: 5 priorities; world stability and "new" international order: 6 priorities)[6].
- Secondly, we identified, by means of scanning of literature, team discussions and opinions from the other services of the Commission and the ACPM members, 8 main

problem-areas:

1. Resources
2. Population
3. Learning
4. Production
5. Life style
6. Social Organisation
7. Technology
8. Ecology.

- _Third_, we listed, on a purely judgemental basis, a number of _potential critical future problems_ for the long term development of the Community within each problem area. From 116 candidate issues we came down to the selection of _22 most critical future issues_ by applying a two steps procedure:

(a) we checked, first, each issue against a set of criteria (the _necessary conditions_ which were all to be satisfied by each issue. Many issues were thus eliminated,

(b) the remaining issues were checked against a second list of criteria (_the discriminating factors_) which were used to rank their degree of criticality.

The 6 _necessary condition_ were

- Relating to European Community goals and objectives
- Being of critical importance in defining options for a European Future
- Aiming at defining R-D-priorities at a European level
- Being within the framework of the priority areas of FAST as defined by the Council
- Suitability for treatment at the Community level
- Being appropriate for being investigated by FAST

(time-, capacity-, finance- and competence- constraints)

The 9 <u>discriminating conditions</u> were

<u>Weight</u>	<u>N</u>^{o}	<u>Criteria</u>
0.20	1	Importance of the impact as measured by the number of people and the severity of the change
0.16	2	High potential impact of the work by FAST
0.16	3	Disparity between projected and preferred situation
0.12	4	Degree to which basic needs are affected
0.12	5	Sensitivity of society, economy, democracy and ecology towards the change
0.08	6	High degree of competence of FAST for looking at the problem
0.08	7	Not being adequately covered by other activities
0.04	8	Adequacy of the existing information base, books, internal and external support
0.04	9	Importance of the impact as measured by the irreversibility and long term nature of the change.

Each "discriminating condition" received an agreed weight factor "g" betwen 0 and 1.

Each project received a priority $0 \le p_{i,n} \le 1$ with respect to the discriminating conditions.

The priority choice for the projects was derived from

$$PC_i = \frac{1}{n} \sum_{(n)} g_i \, p_{i,n}$$

- <u>Fourth</u>, a second round of intensive discussions within the team and with the other Commission services and the ACPM members led to restructuring and grouping the 22 most critical issues and 8 problem areas into <u>7 priority subject areas</u>: i.e.

  1. resources: access to and use
  2. the future of industrial sectors
  3. technology, productivity and employment
  4. social "acceptance" of new technologies
  5. biotechnology
  6. micro-electronics (in the broader sense)
  7. transport and communications.

- <u>Fifth</u>, we then checked "our" 7 priority subject areas with the priority areas defined within the FAST mandate (see <u>figure</u> 1.)

  The comparison showed
    . the primary importance of 2 horizontal cross-links (the future of industrial sectors; the relationship technology-employment),
    . the cruciality of 1 vertical cross-link (the technical change).

4. At that time, our work on <u>L'European mutation</u> was completed. One of the inspiring criteria we used in that work was the assumption that the long term dynamics of a society is characterised by <u>a plurality of the societal times</u>: i.e. major structural variations (adaptations, breakthroughs, crises) cannot be analysed and assessed along one given time horizon (for instance, the year 2000).

Figure 1. Interrelations between the priority areas as defined in the Council of Ministers mandate and the
priority areas as defined by FAST

FAST \ Mandate	Resources	Structural Change	Technical Change	Social Change
Resources: Access and Use	●	•	●	•
The Future of Industrial Sectors	●	●	●	●
Technology, Productivity, Employment	●	●	●	●
Social "Acceptability" of Technical Change	◓	•	●	●
Micro-Electronics (I.T.)	•	●	●	●
Transport-Communications	○	○	◓	○
Biotechnology	●	●	●	•

Strong Relation ● ⟶ ◓ ⟶ ○ ⟶ • Weak Relation

Accordingly, our attention focused on the identification
of the relevant time horizon of the most critical clusters
of problems arising from the major sources of change. Our
conclusions were that

(1)- industrial readjustments within Europe and at inter-
     national level
   - the changing basis of the energy system, and
   - the re-establishment of a compatibility between
     growth, productivity and employment

were the major problems for Europe in the 80ies with deep
implications beyond the 80ies, namely as far as employment
was concerned.

Appropriate R-D options and priorities were not seen as
means for solving these problems in the 80ies (they could
not) but rather as tools for ensuring the necessary requirements for new technological choices and opening the way
to new economic opportunities which could produce their
"positive" effects in the 90ies.

(2) great changes were going to be introduced in almost
    every sphere of human activity by the rapid and wider
    application of micro-electronics-based innovations in
    the 20 coming years.

The information "revolution" is already with us but at its
very beginning. We assumed that the next 20 years will see
"revolution" expanding to its full growth, leading to the
emergence of an "Information Society". Our basic, simple
assumption was that there was not only one probable information society but several possible information societies,
the emerging one in Europe depending on the choice of the
european societies under internal and external constraints.
Three major challenges to the European societies were
identified

- the survival of Europe's economic independence and auto-
nomous capability of innovation

- how to live with the "information society" (need for
anticipating and assessing its broad societal implications)

- how to "manage" the transition towards the desired "information society".

R-D options and priorities were to contribute to the development of a coherent science and technology policy to
ease the European response to such challenges

(3) the recent fundamental progress made in the biological
sciences (the "new biology") were source of a wide
range of new opportunities and potentials for unfore-
seeable developments in the production of desired goods
and services.

Biotechnology was felt destined to be in the coming 30
years a source of technological, economic and social changes, at least comparable (mutatis mutandis) to those associated with information technology.

In this respect, the major problem for the Community seemed
to us to be the elaboration of a European strategy for the
long-term development of biotechnology. Accordingly, R-D
options and priorities were to be identified with a view
to providing the necessary environment and basis for making such a strategy possible and coherent.

5. These conclusions were not only showing a striking conver-
gence with the "messages" concerning the choice of the
priority subject areas that emerged from the described
selection procedure. More significantly, they were pro-

viding a more coherent conceptual framework and clearer specification for the supporting evidence to the high criticality of subject areas such as "the future of industrial sectors", "technology-employment", "technical change", etc. Since long-term issues related to the changing basis and structure of the energy systems were already given a considerably great attention in the member States and within the Commission services, <u>we decided to design our research programme around the identification of R-D options and priorities that could</u>

- have an impact on <u>work and employment</u> in the context of the structural readjustment processes (the major problems for the 80ies).

- contribute to prepare in an appropriate way the emergence of and the transition towards an <u>information society</u> (major change in the 20 coming years).

- help to seize the opportunities offered by <u>biotechnology</u> (the "biosociety") (major change in the 30 coming years).

Thus, the FAST programme was focused on three main unifying themes:

- Work and Employment
- Information Society
- Bio-Society

III. <u>THE CHOICE OF THE RESEARCH PROJECTS</u>

1. Having identified 7 priority subject areas and 3 horizontally unifying themes, we moved next to the choice of the specific research projects with the help of the following

matrix:

Figure 2.

Priority Areas 〳 Horizontally Unifying Themes	1 Access to and Use of Resources	2 The Future of Industrial Sector	3 Technology/Productivity/Employment	4 ...	. 7
General "Problematique"	Possible Relevant Projects	...	...	...	...
Work and Employment	...	Possible Relevant Projects	...	...	...
Information Society	...	...	...	...	...
Bio-Society	...	Possible Relevant Projects	...	...	...

2. A first set of candidate projects were identified by taking into account the team expertise and preferences (to a reasonable extent); the financial resources allocated to each unifying theme; the need to avoid duplication with completed or ongoing research within the Commission services and in the member States, the suggestions and advices from other Comission services and the ACPM members.

Previous work devoted to the definition and the identification of the 22 most critical future issues for the Community provided the required analytical basis for pro-

jects identification in the context of the major "strategic"
issues within each horizontal unifying theme (see <u>figures
3-5)</u>.

3. The end result was the selection of 30 projects

   - 11 projects within <u>Work and Employment</u> sub-programme
   - 7   "   "   <u>Information Society</u> "   "
   - 12   "   "   <u>"Bio-Society"</u>   "   "
   (see <u>figures 3-5</u>)

4. Not all the projects are proper research studies.
   Five projects do imply the preparation and organisation
   of <u>European seminars</u>. The choice of this particular form
   was justified by the nature of the subject choosen, being
   either extremely controversial, or lacking adequate "paradigms" for research type based investigations.

   Two other projects (within the sub-programme "Bio-society")
   were merged into a single exercise: a working group on the
   social dimension of biotechnology.

5. The structural logics by projects of each sub-programme
   is given in <u>figures 3-5</u>.
   The figures show that the final choice of the various projects was not made project by project but by clusters of
   interrelated projects in response to the main crucial
   problems identified <u>within</u> each sub-programme.

Figure 3

FAST WORK AND EMPLOYMENT SUB-PROGRAMME

The research logics and project interrelations

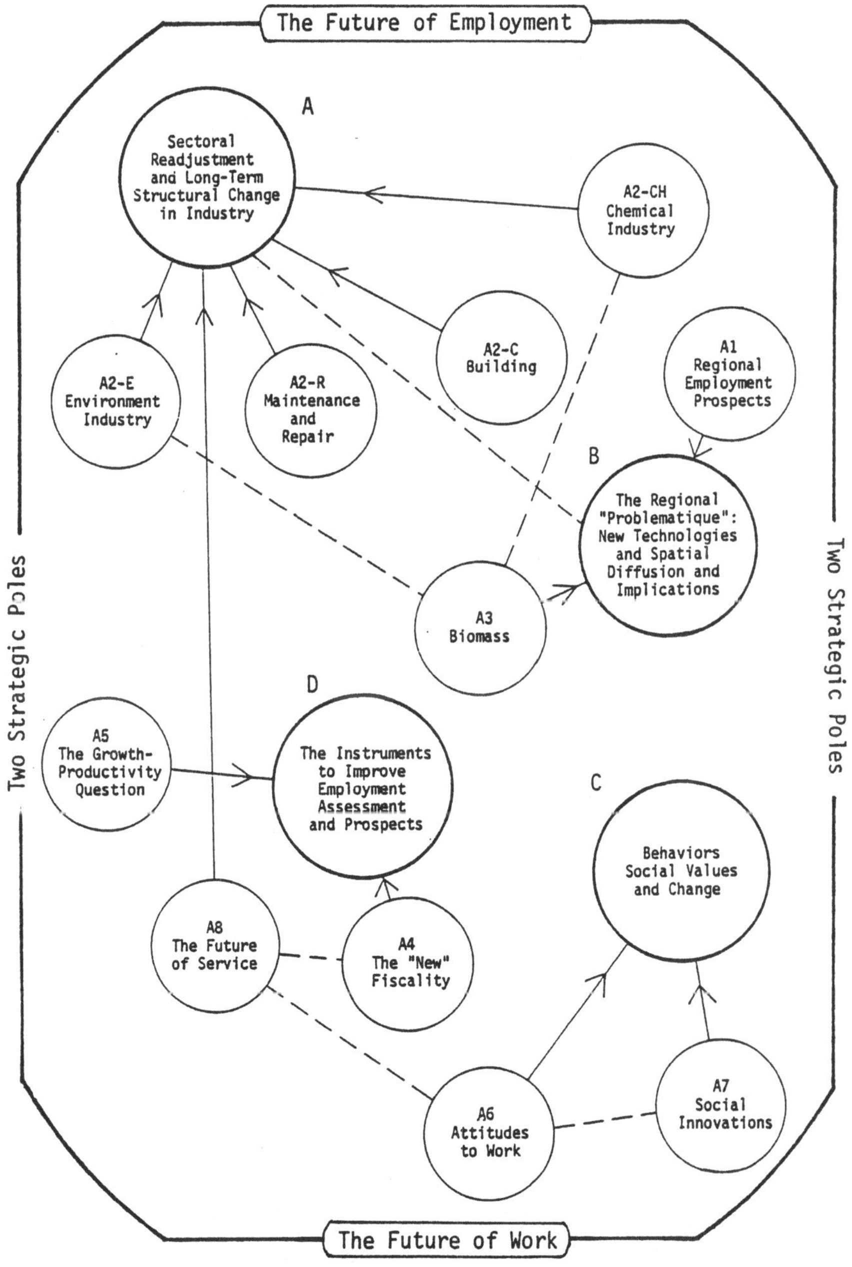

Figure 4

FAST INFORMATION SOCIETY SUB-PROGRAMME
The research logics and project interrelations

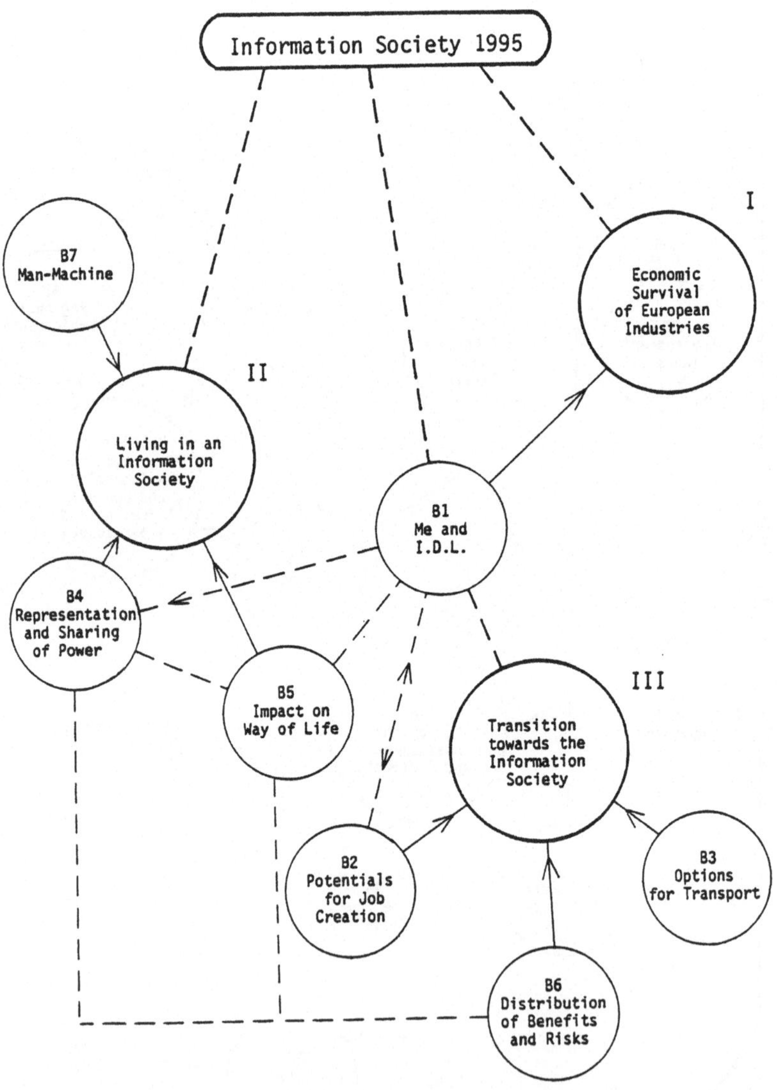

Figure 5

FAST BIO-SOCIETY SUB-PROGRAMME

The research logics and projects interrelations.

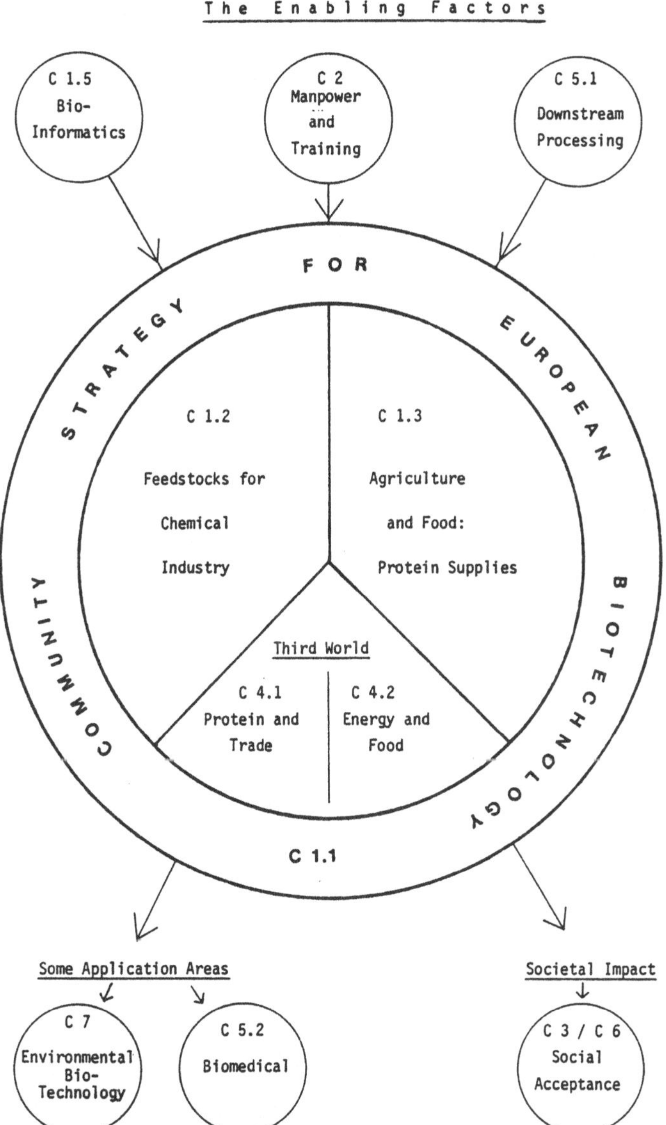

CONCLUDING REMARKS

The three previous sections may give the impression that the team

- adequately managed and "controled" the constraints deriving from the FAST contextual features

- ensured the necessary

    . internal coherence
    . logical sequence
    . rigourous procedures

in the process of programme design and projects choice.

This was what we tried to do. The real story did, however, not include good intentions and achievements only: it was also marked by difficulties and shortcomings. The subjectivity of the actors involved could not (and to my mind was not to) be entirely restrained. Personality factors did play a signi-ficant role, as in any social group dynamics. Objective "judgements" (with the help of quantified techniques) re-mained embodied into (and influenced by) individual or group assumptions, opinions, desires, knowledge, organizational role. This does not mean that the output was necessarily ill-based or inappropriate. It only recognizes the intervention of un-avoidable "biasing" factors.

One basic weakness of the whole exercise was the identifi-cation and definition of the 8 major problem-areas (see above). Though necessary, useful and derived from literature scanning and intensive discussions, such a "list" was an ar-bitrary choice. We, however, accepted it considering that the key element was the appropriate definition of the nature of the <u>specific</u> long-term crucial issues for the Community whatever broad category the various issues could be grouped within.

Some shortcomings did also characterize the use of the <u>discriminating conditions</u> aiming at ranking the respective degree of criticality of those issues that satisfied the necessary conditions. In the course of the exercise, some members of the team renounced using the quantified approach and adopted a more judgemental approach to priority weighting, as they were "troubled" by some surprising results produced by numbers. The confrontation between the list of priority issues established by each team member did, however, permit to correct some inconsistencies and to clear up some conflicting results mostly due to terminology, language and discipline barriers, and in some instances, inadequate definition of the problem. Lack of consensus within the team did also sometimes made full transparence of the priority choice difficult to achieve.

Finally, the interconnections we established between the 7 priority areas and the 3 horizontal unifying themes was more the fruit of team interpretation at a high level of abstraction than the result of self-supporting evidence. Again this does not mean that the output was "wrong" but rather that the interference was not as transparent as it ought to be.

Notes:

(1) FAST: Forecasting and Assessment in the field of Science
    and Technology.

(2) CREST: Comité de la recherche scientifique et technique.

(3) The Social and Economic Committee of the Community and
    the Comité Européen pour la Recherche et la Développement
    (CERD) have also their word to say on the programme.

(4) The Council decision states "the main aim of the research
    programmme is to contribute to the definition of long-
    term Community research and development objectives and
    priorities and thus to the development of a coherent
    science and technology policy in the long-term". In ex-
    plaining the background and rationale for the launching
    of the programme, the Council resolution notes

    - "... extensive research work is being carried out on
      forecasting and assessment at a national level and inter-
      national level, but is not at the present time suffi-
      ciently used by the Community nor specifically tailored
      to the particular problems facing the Community

    - ... the Commission should be granted the capability of
      defining priority areas for R-D action of the Community
      taking into account possible long-term developments and
      of determining the long-term effects of R-D activities
      on the social and economic development of the Community".

(5) The report was published by the Commission of the European
    Community in March 1980. An updatedd version in English,
    Old World and New Technology was published at the be-
    ginning of 1981.

(6) Military security and independence were not included as
    the Community has no competence in this field.

Francois Hetman*

Some Glimpses on the International Co-operation in R&D

*The opinions expressed by the author are his own and do not
necessarily commit the Organisations to which he belongs.

As stated in one of the first OECD reports on science policy, governments can be persuaded to engage in the various forms of international co-operation for one or more of the following considerations:

   i) the research in question (programme, problem, project) is by nature transnational (meteorology, oceanography, etc.);

   ii) it calls for resources on a scale far beyond the means of a single country (nuclear research, space research, etc.);

   iii) it contributes to broader economic and military objectives in pursuit of which countries agree to combine their efforts;

   iv) participation in co-operative action adds to the country's prestige both at home and abroad.[1]

These considerations have a general validity. In the present context, they are complemented by three other reasons for an increased international co-operation:

   a) increased research costs and the levelling off of national expenditures in R&D;

   b) the pressure of problems and challenges common to all countries (energy, national resources, the environment, etc.);

---

1) OECD: Ministers Talk About Science. Paris 1965, pp 79/80.

c) the "transnational" character of many other or new
   research fields which are of concern to most if not
   all Member countries.

Behind all these rather obvious reasons is search for and
acquisition of scientific and technical information at the
lowest cost, not only indirectly measurable in economic terms
but also in terms of general policy and international status
of the country.

There is an important difference between co-operation in
science and fundamental research in particular and co-operation in experimental development and technology.

Since fundamental research is concerned mainly with advance-
ment of knowledge, it seems to be shielded from short-term
urgencies and largely unaffected by economic and political
constraints. Worldwide circulation of ideas is considered as
a precondition of scientific activity and as an inalienable
foundation of the scientific ethics. Most often it is based
on personal contacts or more or less regular meetings orga
nised by associations of scholars and non-governmental bodies. Unrestricted communication and publication of scientific findings have always been considered as the best guarantee of "free research" and its intellectual relevance.

However, full access to the international scientific community is hindered by the very structure of the national research system, its strength and capacity of assimilation and
exploitation of internationally available knowledge. Even
more stringent difficulties arise from the growing dependence
on government funds and the necessity to look for a systematic support within the framework of mission-oriented research.

As far as technological developments are concerned, these

activities are expected to yield findings which will lead to significant economic results and commercial returns on R&D investment. The prevailing tendency is to strengthen national technological capacity and to secure a competitive advantage on international markets. Applied research and experimental development are by definition confidential in nature, carefully imbedded in individual business strategies.

Concentrating on the main trends of multilateral co-operation in intergovernmental organizations, a recent OECD review considers that there has been, particularly in the last decade, a steady development of co-operative research efforts, mainly among the Western European countries. This is shown by the experience of common policy for scientific research and development in the framework of the European Communities on the one hand, and research activities launched under the auspices of OECD and NATO as well as of NORDFORSK for Nordic countries.

With respect to technology three sectors - energy, aviation and space - are most often given as examples of effective international co-operation. These sectors constitute priority areas where policy considerations and, in particular, defence considerations have played a determinant role in supporting and launching R&D activities. Most of the projects are based on bi-lateral agreements.

On the basis of the available experience, a short outline of conditions for intergovernmental co-operation can be drawn up (Table hereafter).

These conditions will be more and more influenced by the general tendency to bring the national R&D effort within a more coherent and purposive relationship with national goals and economic objectives. Many countries take measures to strengthen links between basic research and development, to orientate R&D towards domestically produced processes and to enhance the economic value of R&D findings.

This suggests that national governments will measure, even more than before, their participation in international cooperative ventures in the light of their own needs and opportunities. Within the new economic context they pay increased attention to effectiveness of all components of the R&D system. The emphasis is on a more concrete use of research findings and their direct embodying in new technologies.

This trend towards considering international co-operation in the field of R&D as a highly sophisticated barter of promissing technical developments brings with it a number of caveate for international research on impacts of new technologies.

<u>Political factors</u> - There is no doubt that technology has been a major force in fostering interpenetration of policies and cultures and in creating the present state of interdependence, which seems to commend a coordinated view of world problems. Ideally, innovation energies should be directed towards ensuring that technology increasingly contributes to improving the standard of living and the quality of life both in industrialised and developing countries.
As a matter of fact, technology is far from aiming at the same kind of universality as science. The weight of political factors is rapidly growing as one moves from cooperative enterprises in science to those in technolgy. "As soon as application comes into the picture, the weight of political factors becomes increasingly decisive, since the researchers alone are no longer the sole judges of the nature, of the aim and the value of the results"[1].

---

1) M. Macioti: International Co-operation in Science and Technology. Role for OECD, Paris, October 1971.

CONDITIONS FOR INTERGOVERNMENTAL CO-OPERATION

GENERAL	SPECIFIC TO CO-OPERATION IN SCIENCE	SPECIFIC TO CO-OPERATION IN TECHNOLOGY
Political context: awareness of political implications, programmes in conformity with the interest of the partners	Balance between national and international programmes: complementarity and stimulation	Market research: analysis of market opportunities and capacity and to influence prospective market
Similarity between partners: comparable stage in the scientific and technical development	Training of national experts	Limited number of participants
Clearness of aims: clearly defined at the outset		
Preparatory mechanism: importance of a general mechanism of contact and discussion for launching, defining and mounting joint research ventures		
Institutional framework: defined on the basis of a detailed cost/benefit analysis of the contemplated type of co-operation		A single centre of decision
Structures: preference given to flexible arrangements and mechanisms which allow direct co-operation between national research establishments.	Structures: flexibles and maximum delegation of responsibilities	Integrated participation from drawing-board to execution
Supervision and responsability: monitoring and management function for regular internal programme review	Financial stability: multi-annual-budgets	Responsibility: clear definition of the roles of the public authorities and of industry

<u>Defense</u> <u>of</u> <u>national</u> <u>interests</u> - The balance sheet of the joint undertakings on the inter-governmental level remains subject to opposing opinions. Even if one admits that the first setbacks have been compensated by more carefully structured ventures, the experience shows a number of difficulties in maintaining international commitments.

Aside from intrinsic uncertainties as to the aims of co-operation, the most crucial problem is the unpredictable interpretation and defence of national interests. Joint undertakings may be called into question at any time as the result of a change in policy on the part of one of the participating countries. Moreover, international action adds to its own specific obstacles. What would pass at the national level for an error of management or foresight, will tend to be considered at the international level as a consequence of divergent views among the partners as to the aims, results or sharing of costs and benefits.

<u>Decision-making process</u> - Decisions have to be made between competing and conflicting interests and values. Internalisation of other than direct technical and economic effects implies a change in social and legal structure. This change generates in its turn, its own externalities of psychological, sociological and political nature. It is extremely difficult to perceive and evaluate the full range of problems created at the national level and still more so at the international level where they are compounded and amplified.

As a rule, technology is developed as a trial and error process with opportunities for feedback from social, economic and legal institutions. Such a feedback should allow researchers to modify and reshape a technology and to adapt it better to economic and social objectives. In reality there is little adaption because consequences of a new technological development are difficult to clarify and impossible to

attest objectivly. Moreover, practical and political involvements make it generally difficult to modify the course of
action.This makes decision-makers hesitant and ready to ju-
stify on-going technological trends rather than to challenge
them.

<u>Technology as a competitive advantage</u>. - Technology is more
and more closely linked to nationally organised R&D on the
one side and to a systematic launching of new product lines
on the other. It plays a decisive role in economic efficiency of the country and is considered therefore as the
main source of competive power. As such, it tends to be sur-
rounded by walls of secrecy during the phase of development,
and by patents and licences when ready for the market.

The "social cost" of developing new technologies varies from
country to country. Its minimization in current business
calculations is often due to specific government measures or
fiscal alleviations. This may raise problems of distorting
the established pattern of international exchange of goods.

Joint international undertakings happen to be suspected to
bear a risk of reducing the competitive force of national
firms. An attitude of 'laissez-aller' can thus be justified
on the grounds that each country is compelled to leave technology proliferate for the sake of the national survival.

<u>Institutional gap.</u> - Research on impacts of new technologies
is a new concept and a new approach to technological change
in liasion with general policy. The major obstacle to international co-operation in this field, and in that of technology in general, is the absense of technology policy as
such and government body responsible for it.

R&D policy has taken as a model big mission-oriented organizations where R&D activities are combined to aim at a given
objective (nuclear, space, missiles, energy, etc.) This

objective (nuclear, space, missiles, energy, etc.) This implies an organizational merger of fundamental research, applied research and experimental development. Taking roughly R for science and D for technology, national governments and international organizations adopted the term science and technology policy for a complex of activities which include in fact only some premises of technology policy.

However, from the institutional point of view technology does not have its own status. There is a wide dispersion of competences among the various ministries and agencies. Each of these is responsible for only one aspect of a given technology. They are thus hampered by their statutory responsibilities and particularly so in matters of international co-operation.

ABOUT THE AUTHORS

<u>Niels Bjørn-Andersen</u> is Associate Professor at the Infor-
mation Systems Research Group, Copenhagen Business School.
He earned his Ph.D. in the field of management information
systems from the Copenhagen Business School and an MBA in
Business Administration and Industrial Sociology. In 1972 -
1974 he was appointed Head of the Institute of Organization
and Industrial Sociology, Copenhagen Business School. At
Manchester Business School he was Visiting Researcher from
1974 - 1975, and in 1980 Visiting Professor at Paris Uni-
versité IX Dauphine.

<u>Vary T. Coates</u> has been Adjunct Professor at The George
Washington University since 1976 and Adjunct Associate
Professor at Carnegie Mellon University (Pittsburgh) since
1979. She graduated from Furman University (in 1951) with
a B.A. in Political Science, with a M.A. at The George
Washington University (in 1969), and her Ph.D. thesis
("Technology and Public Policy") was accepted in 1972. She
received a D. Sc. (Hon.) at Webster College in 1973. She
was President of the International Society for Technology
Assessment (ISTA) 1975 - 76. She was Associate Director
within the Program of Policy Studies in Science & Technology at The George Washington University until 1978. From
1978 - 1979 she was Associate Director within the Technology Assessment Division, Office of Technology Impacts,
U.S. Department of Energy. From 1978 - 1981 she was Director
in the Policy Analysis & Technology Assessment Department of
Dames & Moore and is now Vice President, J.F. Coates Inc.
Professor Coates has been a consultant to a number of institutes and administrations. She is the author of "Retrospective Assessment: Submarine Telegraphy - Transatlantic Cable
of 1866", and of numerous articles.

Francois Hetman is a principal administrator with the OECD Directorate for Science, Technology and Industry in Paris. He has a Ph.D. in economic science and is specialized in economic growth problems, science and technology policy and futures research. He is author of several books among which are Europe of Abundance, Secrets of the American Giants, The Language of Forecasting, Mastering the Future, Society and the Assessment of Technology, Science Policy Formats, Methods of Technological Forecasting, and of a number of articles.

Ida R. Hoos is Research Sociologist at the Space Sciences Laboratory of the University of California, Berkeley. A graduate of Radcliffe, she received her Ph.D. in Sociology in 1959. Her publications include a number of journal articles and the following books: Automation in the Office (1961); Retraining the Workforce (1967); and Systems Analysis in Public Policy (1972). She has served as a member of the National Academy of Sciences Committee on Energy Storage, the Nuclear Regulatory Commission's panel on Nuclear Waste Management, the National Science Foundation's Directorate on Science, Technology, and International Affairs, and the U.S. Congressional Office of Technology Assessment (U.S. Civilian Space Policy). Her research subjects include technology assessment, risk analysis, and systems methodology.

G. Patrick Johnson is since 1974 Senior Policy Analyst at the National Science Foundation in Washington, D.C.. Previously he was a consultant to SRI International and RAND Corporation, as well as INTASA Inc., and Institute for Water Resources, U.S. Army Corps of Engineers at National Science Foundation. Dr. Johnson is working with Technology Assessment and Risk Analysis Group (Division of Policy Research and Analysis). His alma maters are the University of Missisippi (B.S.) and Stanford University (M.S. and Ph.D.).

<u>Horstfried Läpple</u> has been employed at Bayer AG in Leverku-
sen (Federal Republic of Germany) since 1980. He received the
M.S. degree in engineering-economics in 1978. He was a Research
Associate in the Department of Business Administration and
Operations Research at the Technische Hochschule Darmstadt,
where he completed his Ph.D. thesis in 1978. At Stanford
University he worked from 1978 - 1979 as a Postdoctoral Fellow
in the Department of Engineering-Economic Systems.

<u>Bernd-Peter Lange</u> is Professor of economics at the Univer-
sity of Osnabrück (Federal Republic of Germany). He received
a diploma in economics and a Ph.D. in jurisprudence. He was
a member of the commission for the development of the technical
communication system and published in the field of the development of economic concentration, and media policy.

<u>Renate Mayntz</u> is Professor of sociology at the University
of Cologne. She obtained a B.A. from Wellesley College, a
doctorate in sociology at the Free University in Berlin,
honorary doctorates from the Universities of Uppsala and
Paris. Before going to the University of Cologne, she has
held chairs at the Free University in Berlin and the Hochschule für Verwaltungswissenschaften in Speyer. She has
taught at Columbia University and the New School of Social
Research in New York, at the University of Edinburgh and
at FLACSO (Facultad Latino-Americana de Ciencas Sociales),
Santiago de Chile. Together with F.W. Scharpf she published
"Policy-making in the German Federal Bureaucracy". In 1978
she published a book on the sociology of public administration. Upon request of the Federal Ministry of the Interior
Prof. Mayntz finished a scientific interpretation about
"Legislation and Bureaucracy" in 1980.

<u>Peter Mertens</u> is Professor for business data processing at the University of Erlangen-Nuremberg since 1970. He is a member of the board of the Regional Computing Center, Erlangen, since 1974. Prof. Mertens has worked in Economic and Business Administration Departments of the Universities of Darmstadt and Munich and thereafter as a vice-president for a leading EDP consulting firm in Switzerland. In 1968 he became a full professor for Industrial Engineering at the University of Linz, Austria. His main research activities are in computer-assisted information and planning systems and in EDP applications in production planning and accounting.

<u>Herbert Paschen</u> is the head of the Department for Applied System Analysis of the Nuclear Research Centre, Karlsruhe (Federal Republic of Germany). His Ph.D. was in economics. He has been a faculty member at the University of Heidelberg. At the Centre Européen de Formation des Statisticiens-Economistes des Pays en Voie de Développement (CESD) in Paris, he has been a vice-manager. He has served as a consultant to OECD, the European Community and to UNESCO in matters related to Technological Forecasting and Technology Assessment. His publications concern Systems Analysis, Planning of Research and Development and Technology Assessment.

<u>Riccardo Petrella</u> is Head of the FAST programme (Forecasting and Assessment in the field of Science and Technology) within the Commission of the European Community. From 1971-1976 he was Director of the European Coordination Centre for Research in the Social Science in Vienna (Austria); from 1976-1978 he was Senior Research Fellow at the International Social Science Council (Paris) under a Ford Foundation grant and Consultant to the Commission of the European Communities in the field of social science research. Since 1976 he has

also been lecturing at the Faculty of Economics at University of Namur. He received a Dr. Fil (Hon) at the University of Umeo (Sweden) in 1975. His publications include several books, in particular dealing with regional and industrial location problems in Europe.

<u>Michael Rader</u> is a member of a research team at the Karlsruhe Nuclear Research Centre, Federal Republic of Germany, investigating the effects of the application of computer-aided design. He received his Ph.D. in sociology from Hamburg University. He has previous professional experience with a firm of consultants in housing and town planning and has been with the Department of Applied Systems Analysis at the Nuclear Research Centre since 1979.

<u>Jürgen Reese</u> is Professor at the University in Kassel (Federal Republic of Germany). He holds the M.A. and Ph.D. degrees in sociology. At the Gesellschaft für Mathematik und Datenverarbeitung (GMD) he works as a Visiting Scientist in the Institute for Planning and Decision Support Systems. Prof. Reese has also served as Visiting Lecturer at the University in Bochum. In the fields of planning organization, political communication and information influenced by dataprocessing he published several articles and books.

<u>Ursula M. Richter</u> is researcher and leader of projects on conceptual questions of research on impacts of information technologies and on office automation at the Institute for Organisation and Automation (BIFOA) at the University of Cologne since 1980. She received her diploma of business administration in 1974 and her Ph.D. in 1978 at the University of Cologne. Since 1974 she was there research assistant. In 1979-1980 she was Postdoctorial Fellow of IBM at the Research Laboratory in San Jose.

<u>Norbert Szyperski</u> is Chairman of the Board of Executives of the Gesellschaft für Mathematik und Datenverarbeitung (GMD), Professor of Business Administration and Business Planning at the University of Cologne, and Director at the Institute for Organization and Automation (BIFOA) at the University of Cologne. He attended the Free University of Berlin and received a diploma in business administration, and his Ph.D. thesis was accepted there in 1962. Since 1958 he was research assistant at the Free University of Berlin. In 1962 he got a fellowship of the Eisenhower Exchange Program in Philadelphia, USA. Hereafter he was Assistant Professor of Management at the University of Florida in Gainsville. He has written a number of books and articles and is editor (with E. Grochla) of "Information Systems and Organizational Structure", "Design and Implementation of Computer-based Information Systems", and of several journals.

<u>Bernd Wingert</u> is leader of a project dealing with the effects of the application of computer-aided design carried out at the Nuclear Research Centre in Karlsruhe (Federal Republic of Germany). He holds a diploma in psychology from the University of Heidelberg (1972). During his university studies, his special interest was in theoretical and social psychology. Afterwards he worked for several years at the Studiengruppe für Systemforschung in Heidelberg. Since 1975 he has been with the Department for Applied System Analysis at the Nuclear Research Centre, Karlsruhe.

PARTICIPANTS

BERGER, Wolfram Götz, Dr.	Bundesministerium für Wirtschaft, Bonn
BIHL, Volker, Dr.	Bundesministerium des Innern, Bonn
BJØRN-ANDERSEN, Niels, Prof. Dr.·	Copenhagen School of Economics and Business Administration, Kopenhagen
BÜTTGENBACH, Hans-Peter	Dipl.-Oec., BIFOA, Köln
COATES, Vary T., Prof. Dr.	George Washington University, Washington, D.C.
EISENBEIß, Gerd, Dr.	Bundesministerium für Forschung und Technologie, Bonn
FAUSER, Albrecht	M.A., Fraunhofer Institut für Arbeitswirtschaft und Organisation, Stuttgart
FISCHER, Gerhard Dr.	Universität Stuttgart, Institut für Informatik, Stuttgart
GLÄSS, Siegfried	IBM Deutschland GmbH, Stuttgart

GROCHLA, Erwin,   Universität zu Köln,
Prof. Dr. Dr. h.c. mult.   BIFOA, Köln

HAEFNER, Klaus, Prof. Dr.   Universität Bremen,
                                         Bremen

HANSEN, Hans   Dipl.-Ing., DATUM e.V.,
                                         Bonn

HEIMANN, Walter   Dipl.-Ing., Siemens AG,
                                         Bonn

HÖRING, Klaus   Dipl.-Ing.,Dipl.-Wirtsch.
                                         -Ing., BIFOA, Köln

HOOS, Ida, Dr.   University of California,
                                         Berkeley

JOHNSON, G. Patrick, Dr.   National Science Founda-
                                         tion, Washington, D.C.

KOCHS, Hubert   GMD-APM, Birlinghoven

LÄPPLE, H., Dr.   Köln

LANGE, B.-P., Prof. Dr.   Universität Osnabrück

LANGE, Siegfried, Dr.   Fraunhofer-Institut für
                                         Systemtechnik und Innova-
                                         tionsforschung, Karlsruhe

LANGENHEDER, Werner, Dr.   GMD, Birlinghoven

LOEBEN, Manfred — Dipl.-Kfm., Gesellschaft für Information und Dokumentation, Sektion für Systementwicklung, Heidelberg

MACHNIK, Johannes — Dipl.-Kfm., GMD-APM, Birlinghoven

MANZ, Ulrich — Dipl.Verw.Wiss., Hochschule der Bundeswehr, München

MAROCK, Jürgen, Dr. — GMD-APM, Birlinghoven

MARWEDEL, Henning — Datenzentrale Schleswig-Holstein, Kiel

MAYNTZ, Renate, Prof. Dr. Dr. h.c. mult. — Universität zu Köln, Köln

MERTENS, Peter, Prof. Dr. — Universität Erlangen/Nürnberg, Erlangen

PASCHEN, Herbert, Dr. — Kernforschungszentrum Karlsruhe, Karlsruhe

PETRELLA, Riccardo, Dr. — Commission of the European Communities, Brüssel

POOR, Josef, Dr. — Universität Pécs, Ungarn

REESE, Jürgen, Prof. Dr. — Gesamthochschule Kassel, Kassel

RICHTER, Ursula, Dr.   BIFOA, Köln

SCHMIDT, Herbert, Dr.   Bundesministerium für
                                        Arbeit und Sozialordnung,
                                        Bonn

SZYPERSKI, Norbert, Prof. Dr.   Universität zu Köln,
                                        BIFOA, Köln

TAKAHASHI, Hiroyuki, Prof.   Soka University, Tokyo

VÖGE, K.-H., Dr.   Nixdorf Computer AG,
                                        Berlin

VOLPERT, P., Prof. Dr.   Technische Universität
                                        Berlin, Institut für
                                        Humanwissenschaft in
                                        Arbeit und Ausbildung,
                                        Berlin

WEITZ, Wilfried P.,   Dipl.-Kfm., BIFOA, Köln

WINGERT, Bernd   Dipl.-Psych., Kernfor-
                                        schungszentrum Karlsru-
                                        he, Karlsruhe

WIßKIRCHEN, Peter, Dr.   GMD-IIG, Birlinghoven

ZAHN, Erich, Prof. Dr.   Universität Stuttgart,
                                        Betriebswirtschaftliches
                                        Institut, Stuttgart

ZORN, Werner   Dipl.-Vw., IBM Deutsch-
                                        land GmbH, Stuttgart